THE SECRETS & SEDUCTIONS

OF LIVING IN THE MIDDLE EAST

DR. THERESA BROWN

DEDICATION

This book is dedicated to my parents, Sandra L. Turner, and Larry H. Williams for always believing in me and never giving up on me.

My children, Chelsea, and Rylan for showing how my parents must've felt when they realized I too had a mind of my own.

To my siblings, Territa, Tawania, and Larry, thanks for always making me feel bigger than life itself. I love you all.

TABLE OF CONTENTS

INTRODUCTION

Shuffling through the Atlanta airport with five oversized mix matched suitcases and sweat beads dripping down my face was not what I expected on my departure. I tripped over my bags three times before making my way to the counter to check in for my one-way ticket to Abu Dhabi, United Arab Emirates. I nervously checked my purse three times to make sure I had Chelsea and I passports and my work visa. My daughter Chelsea met me at the airport with her dad, brother, uncle, and cousin. My six-year-old son was in rare form. He hit his younger female cousin in the face. He wasn't listening to me or his dad. He had a mean frown on his face as he walked his sister and me to the security line to head to our gate. I knew part of his aggression was because he wanted to go with us, and I wanted him to go as well. I felt really bad because I knew it would be months before I would see him again.

I really wanted him to go with us, but his dad refused to let him go. This was a turning point in my life and I didn't want to experience it without my two kids.

Life takes on many twists and turns and how you navigate through them can make you stronger or lead you down a road of depression. I had to figure out how to handle a failed marriage and the death of my mother while learning to love me at the same time. Both took me on a rollercoaster of life's peaks and valleys. If you asked me five years ago where I saw myself in life or what I would be doing in life, traveling the world and being a school administrator in the middle east to looking for a job to becoming an entrepreneur would not have been my answer. There were traumatic events that took place in my life that led me down a path of self-discovery and an increased relationship with the most important soul in my life, me.

"You are where you thought you would be" is a quote that has me constantly thinking, what the hell was I thinking years ago that brought me to this point in my life. I am divorced, a mother of two kids, educator, an entrepreneur, motherless child, and still trying to figure my way through life. Moving to the middle east has played a large role in helping me discover who I am and how I can be more compassionate and forgiving to me. The process of discovering who I truly am and who I want to be is a gruesome and lonely process.

Especially when the process begins seven thousand miles away from my family and friends, I've known all my life, in a place that is completely opposite of my normalcy.

It was like I had to go halfway across the world to learn how to be still and how to appreciate time alone. When I first moved to the United Arab Emirates it was as if my body was there, but my mind was still in the United States. I constantly longed for the busy life I was used to having in the United States. I didn't know how to be still or alone with my thoughts.

I hadn't planned to document my experience living in the middle east and definitely didn't expect to see and hear about some of the things I saw and heard. There were secrets that the world didn't know existed about the middle east. I was seduced in a way that made me become a totally different person. My views on the Muslim culture and Ramadan would never be the same. The month of Ramadan changed my life forever.

CHAPTER 1

THE BEGINNING

Losing a parent or child can be one of the hardest and, by far, one of the most emotional experiences one could endure. Imagine slowly losing your mother to cancer and going through a divorce at the same time. I never thought in a million years that I would see my mother's health deteriorate right before my very eyes. There wasn't a thing I could do to save "Sandra Turner", as her closest friends called her. For some reason, they loved saying her full name whenever they spoke of Momma. She was truly the life of not just the party, but the work environment, school environment, even the political party meetings for which she was a volunteer. My mother never met a stranger.

I remember growing up and my mom taking me shopping or just to run errands, she would always run into somebody she knew. She was so personable with people. She had an infectious smile and a natural body shape that is now made in plastic surgeons' offices. My mom had an hour glass shape. Her milkshake would bring all the boys to the yard. Now to see this vibrant woman crippled and stripped of her livelihood to lung cancer was heartbreaking. My mother who was 5'11 and weighed over 200 pounds was now frail with sagging skin and her bones were visible through her thin translucent skin due to the disease. Her cancer-stricken body was barely 145 pounds, and the Coca-Cola bottle shape figure no longer existed.

I wasn't shocked when I found out Momma had lung cancer. She smoked cigarettes all her life. Anytime someone tried to encourage her to give up smoking, she would boast, "Shit, I been smoking since I was 12 years old." Every time she said that, I imagined this little fast-tail girl sneaking into the bathroom smoking cigarettes with some other little girls. My mom was not a typical kid. She sneaked out of the house, hitchhiked rides, and attended rent parties way before she even started her period. If you're from a younger generation, a rent party is when you throw a house party and charge people to get in to earn enough money to pay the rent. Today, you would be considered a party promoter. I learned these stories about her through my aunt. Anytime my mom would scold my sisters and me for wanting to do something outside of the house, my Aunt Jean, who was a couple years older than my mother, would interrupt with a crazy childhood story about my mom. For instance, Aunt Jean loved telling us about the times Momma would sneak out of the house to go to concerts, meet grown men, and do all kinds of things she wasn't supposed to do as a teenager. She tried her best to shield us girls from her adolescence, but we all knew she lived a fast life.

When my mom called me in December to tell me she had a lump on her chest, I was nervous. My heart began beating fast. I immediately thought, "Please God, don't let it be cancerous." I was home alone in my two-bedroom apartment when I got the news. I'd been living there for two years after separating from my husband. I was sure the marriage was done. It became more apparent during the time of my mother's illness. We learned the tumor was cancerous on my mother's 67th birthday. She had stage 4 lung cancer. My mother had been complaining for the past three months that she was always tired. In retrospect, it seemed like she had never felt good lately. My niece convinced her to see a respiratory specialist. She had been using an inhaler for six months prior to her diagnosis. Her family doctor prescribed it to her to help with her breathing. Two of my sisters had asthma so she thought it was asthma. I was shocked with fear and hurt. Hearing the news struck fear in my heart. I immediately thought, "I don't want to lose momma." I'd wished I lived closer to home. I was getting ready to purchase a plane ticket home from Conyers, Georgia, which is just outside of Atlanta. On her instructions not to, I changed my mind and stayed where I was. They hadn't decided on a treatment plan anyway, so I wouldn't have known how to take care of her. However, a couple months after Christmas, I flew home to care for her.

When I arrived to see my mother for the first time, her living room had been transformed into a makeshift hospital room with a hospital bed and a small television inches away from the foot of her bed. The front door was unlocked. She could hear me entering because the bottom of the screen door scraped against the cement finished threshold as I opened it. The house reeked of formaldehyde, rubbing alcohol, and moth balls. My stomach knotted up as soon as I walked through the door of her two-bedroom townhouse on the eastside of Detroit. The family pictures remained on the hallway walls and in the kitchen as they were the last time I was there. The refrigerator was full of magnets. There were magnets from vacation cities, funny sayings, and more. Her house reminded me of an old grandma, but I never thought of my mother as old.

As I entered the house there were pictures of 20 years past hanging along the wall to the staircase that led to the bedrooms. She loved collecting pictures of family graduations, prom dates, and various family portraits. My mother loved to display family pictures. She stopped giving my father pictures of us as kids because he never put them up in his house. To this day, my dad still doesn't have family pictures displayed in his house, and I keep mine for my personal spaces in my home. I walked down the hallway to where she was sitting up in her hospital bed which now occupied the space where her rectangular marble dining room table used to be. Her gray, thin hair was combed to the back of her head barely grazing her neck. Her hair was so thin that you could see her scalp. She smiled and greeted me with the little energy she had left, "Hey, Baby Girl!" I wanted to cry, but I put a smile on and gave my mother a hug and said, "Hey, ma."

As I took care of my mom, she would cry and scream about the pain of cancer. I remember helping my mom move from the hospital bed to the reclining chair, so I could change the linen on the bed and she would wail and cry, "The pain is too much" she would say in a trembling voice. At the same time, she would apologize for not being able to take care of herself. "Baby Girl, I'm so sorry. I wish I could do this. I'm so tired." My mother said the pain of cancer was unbearable and indescribable. She called out many times, "Jesus! Just take me away!" Seeing my mother in pain hurt my soul. I couldn't believe that she couldn't bathe herself, go to the bathroom on her own anymore, much less do any of the things she liked to do. This was my first time being around anyone that was fighting cancer. My mother was dying and there was nothing I could do about it. I knew my mother did not want to die. She wanted to live life her way as she always had. She never took advice from friends or family. She was the main one always giving advice. It was like she really had a mind of her own and could care less what other people thought about her.

My mom had to grow up fast due to some adult decisions she made as a kid. She had her first child at 15 years old, with others following when she was 17, 19, 21, 27 and finally her last born when she was 30. Yes, my mom had six kids by the time she was 30 years old. Her oldest child, my brother Tracey, was raised by my grandparents. My mother grew up in a two-parent household and was a teenage mother. Just because both parents live in the home doesn't stop teenage pregnancy. My mother raised her other 5 children on her own. My oldest sister and fourth sister had the same father. My youngest brother and I had the same father. My mother had six kids by four different men. She always worked and provided for us the best way she could. She raised us to live life without her. She always talked about our being independent and not depending on others for help. "You need to get a job or go to somebody's college," she would always say. "You got to go at 18." My mother did not believe in taking care of grown people, which is probably why she had such a hard time with my sisters and I taking care of her battling a terminal illness.

One day, I was driving my mother home after one of her doctor's visits. She looked like she had been in a fight with a bear. I guess you could say she was fighting a treacherous bear named Cancer. Her clothes didn't fit anymore and hung off her now frail thin body. She lost about 40 pounds in one month. She was tired. Her face was drooping and the darkness under her eyes was taking over her sunken face. She turned to me as she held back tears and said, "I don't want to die at 67, but I lived a good life." I could see her thinking about the past years. She continued to say, "I got to see all my children grow up and saw their children grow up." It was like she knew her life expectancy was getting shorter. I too held back the tears and tried to look confident. My mom continued, "I got to travel with you" with a soft smile on her face. The thought must have brought a sense of happiness. "I lived a good life" mom said with more confidence.

I didn't want my momma to die either. She was supposed to be at my kids' high school graduation. I had always envisioned my mom screaming at my children's high school graduation, especially my daughter's graduation. She loved Chelsea. I think it's because they were so much alike. Chelsea and my mother are the type of people that are determined to live life their way and forget what others think. My father would say that I'm like that, too. My dad would always point out the confident and tenacious characters in me. I love talking to him because he reminded me of my inner strength that I possessed.

My mother died three months later the 14th of April. Going through this experience forced me to seriously reflect and reevaluate my life as a daughter, sister, mother, and wife. I guess you can say that her death was the catalyst for my life. I kept thinking *damn there are so many things that I want to do that I haven't even scratched the surface to do*. I constantly thought to myself, *this can't be my life right now*. I thought I had plans for my life, but really, I was just going through the motions of living. My marriage was on its last leg, and my spouse was not the most supportive during the period in which I still had to fulfill my professional duties as a school administrator, and mother of very active children. After my mother died, I had been separated from my husband for close to three years. I was constantly dealing with the stresses of working in Atlanta Public Schools, running my daughter to swim practice four days a week, working part-time for an online university, trying to spend time with my emotional 4-year-old son, and get in a date with some handsome fellow. My close friends that knew all my emotional breakdowns of losing my mom and divorcing the man I'd been with since I was 19 years old was taking its toll on me.

I tried to self-medicate myself with wine, but I was getting fat and not feeling any better. Then I tried to shop myself to wellness. I would fall asleep with shoes and clothes in my shopping cart on the websites of Nordstrom, Victoria Secrets, Saks, Macys, Target, you name it. Sometimes I would receive packages in the mail of things I couldn't remember ordering. The shopping was getting out of hand. I still didn't feel any better, and my credit card bills were steadily increasing right along with my weight. I even tried to date to make myself feel better. However, I think the men could see that I was an emotional wreck and were not trying to be caught up in the mix. I was on a battlefield with life disturbed with emotional conflict and pain.

I later learned, through years of therapy, that looking for things of the external world is not going to make you feel better nor will it bring you happiness or sustain your happiness within. You must look deep inside yourself and acknowledge your true emotions, feelings, all of which make you, you. This can be done alone, or you can do like I did—find a damn good therapist. I think at one time, therapy wasn't something people in the black community immediately embraced. Things are a lot different now. In fact, I found that a lot of black women were attending therapy sessions when I was going to therapy.

I found that my therapist was the one person that did not have any expectations of me nor did he want anything from me. He would suggest that I read various books. I learned that events in a person's childhood between the ages of 9 and 14 are very crucial in how they make decisions as an adult. I think events and a child's upbringing between the ages of 5-17 has an enormous impact on the decisions they make as adults. I say that because of the high school seniors I worked with that made bad decisions their senior year in high school that impacted their life in a major way. So, my life decision to move abroad as a single black mother of two was the result of truly seeking to find out who I was, who I wanted to be, and how I could become the person God designed and intended me to be. I vacillated with the idea over and over in my head. I didn't ask the opinions of others because I knew it would cloud my decision. I loved to travel, but the fear of being far away from home and a totally new job in a world I didn't know brought a sense of curiosity and adventure. I needed a change of scenery. My job at the time helped make that decision.

I've been in education for twenty years. My first teaching job began when I was a kindergarten teacher in Stone Mountain, Georgia in Dekalb County School System. I now realize this position was truly ordained by God. I am still very close friends with many of the ladies I worked with at Dunaire Elementary School. It was my first teaching job at what would become one of my favorite schools. I would consider us to be "old school" teachers. "Old School" teacher means a veteran teacher from previous decades, back in the day. They weren't like the teachers of today. We didn't try to be Facebook and Instagram friends with our students. We cared about our students and did whatever it took to ensure that they succeeded at learning. We'd be damned if we allowed the teacher the following year to look at us crazy because we sent them students that knew absolutely nothing. We were teachers that stayed late planning and preparing for authentic teaching and learning, not following a script. My principal was a no-nonsense kind of leader. To this day, my friends and I laugh about how she wanted to send me home for wearing fitted capris at a Saturday carnival. I refused to go home to change my pants. My principal was known for placing a post-it notes in a teacher's mailbox that stated, "See Me." If a teacher received this note, he or she knew something was going down. We were the kind of teachers that could party all night and still teach our butts off the next morning. Educating others was our real passion.

My friends still tease me to this day about the time I called my principal at home while she was sick to tell her that the Assistant Principal would not allow me to give awards to my impressionable Kindergarteners during the school award ceremony. The criteria for Honor Roll and Principal's List was changed from that day forward to include Kindergarteners. I would go to battle if necessary for my students. My first year's students have careers and are married and have children of their own today.

Enough about my first years of teaching. The point I made earlier is that there was something about teaching and the childhood experiences that we endure. When the opportunity came along for me to work as an administrator in another country after going through a messy divorce and losing my mother to lung cancer, I had to accept the job offer. That was the only choice I could've made at that time.

I never knew the opportunity was going to happen like it did, but you never know what God's plans are until you trust him. During one of my walks at Stone Mountain Park with my sorority sister Deirdre, I had expressed interest in working as an educator overseas. I love traveling. Living in the middle of the world would give me an opportunity to travel and experience other cultures. I would finally get to see what the other side of the world was all about. Deirdre and I walked around Stone Mountain Park regularly during the summer. It was a good way for us to swap stories about the school drama, bounce ideas off each other and lose weight at the same time. She also expressed interest in working abroad. She and I both knew a couple people that worked in the United Arab Emirates who had really liked the experience.

As I was getting ready for school one morning, my cell phone rang. It had to be about 6 o'clock in the morning. No one calls me that early in the morning unless it's my parents calling me on my birthday or there was an urgent message. Deirdre was calling to tell me that she had given an overseas teacher recruiter my name and number and that he would be calling me today to see if I was interested in working overseas.

That's just like a friend that will give your number and then tell you they gave your number out to a stranger. I didn't know it at the time, but Deirdre's impulsive action would change my life.

CHAPTER 2

THE INTERVIEW

Deirdre and I left the night of February 13, 2017, to drive to Charlotte, North Carolina, where my cousin and his family lived nearby. My cousin agreed to let us stay at his house overnight. From their house, it would only take us about thirty minutes to get to the location of the interviews, which were conducted on Valentine's Day. We felt like it was a good sign because it was the same day as our line anniversary. This was our 8th year being a part of the sorority. We were both interviewing for a position to work in the United Arab Emirates (UAE). We both knew a couple of people that already lived and worked there, and they encouraged us to try it out. The interviews took place via Skype which is interesting because now the UAE disapproves the use of Skype. The interviews included people from all over the United States. We were told to bring original copies of our passport, teaching certificate, and five passport photos. We had to wake up extra early to find a CVS or Walgreens, so Deirdre could get passport pictures taken because she had forgotten hers in Atlanta. In addition to bringing the necessary documents, we had to ensure that we were dressed appropriately. We had to wear something that covered our legs to the ankle and covered our arms that extended beyond our elbows.

Deirdre and I were damn near dressed like twins. We both had on long black maxi skirts, white collar shirts with a black blazer over the crisp white shirts. She wore pearl earrings and a pearl necklace while I wore a black and white printed scarf. When we arrived at the hotel just outside of Charlotte, there were about 100 other people interviewing for teaching and administrative positions. Everyone was professionally dressed. A couple of ladies had on short skirts, which was totally inappropriate for the interview based on the culture and customs of the country. In preparation for that interview, I learned that you must wear clothing that covers your ankles and tops that come past your elbows when conducting school business in the middle east.

I saw several other people that were employed by Atlanta Public Schools. I spotted another administrator that was in a cohort for aspiring principals in Atlanta. We both smiled at each other as if to say, "I want something better too." The interview process began in a large ballroom of a hotel.

Someone gave us the run-down of what would happen before the actual interview via skype with UAE school personnel. They made it clear that the positions were not in Dubai. We were told that if we were hired we could be placed in any of the Abu Dhabi regions. Abu Dhabi covered a large area of UAE. It's one of the largest Emirates in UAE. The people that lived and worked in Abu Dhabi said that because I had children, I would probably be placed in the Al Ain region, which was known for having families with children. There were other regions such as Abu Dhabi City and the West Region. Abu Dhabi City was the main city and the West Region was hours away from Abu Dhabi City. It would be considered rural. Al Ain was only 1 hour and 30 minutes from Abu Dhabi City. The interviews took place about ten o'clock in the morning which meant that it was about six or seven o'clock in the evening in the UAE.

When my name was called by a recruiter, my stomach started to jump like kids were playing hopscotch inside. I instantly became nervous. My head started spinning and I began to perspire above my top lip. I really didn't know why I was nervous; I had gone through a lot of education interviews during my career. I was escorted by a male recruiter whom I learned was filling in for the recruiter I had been dealing with up to this point. My recruiter was supposed to be there, but something happened with his flight.

I sat down at a long table in front of a computer. On the computer screen were two gentlemen sitting at a long table in front of a microphone. They both gave me a cordial greeting. The interviewers asked basic questions about my experience as an educator. However, there were a few questions that caught me off-guard, mainly because these questions would never be asked in an American interview. One of the questions was, "Are you married?" I said that I was divorced. I had only been divorced 14 days, but when I verbalized it at the interview, it felt kind of good to know that I was over a rough patch in my life. At least I thought I was over a rough patch. Life has a way of showing many rough patches. After living in a Muslim country, I learned that it is better to be divorced than to have never married at all when you have children. Women that had children and not married was looked down upon and wasn't considered as a family. The country didn't recognize one of my friends that had kids and unmarried as a family, so our housing allowances were different. One of my friends even thought about getting married so she could get more housing allowances from the education government. In the UAE, it is against the law to have children when one is not married. The next intrusive question had to do with my religion. "What is your religion?" asked the interviewer. Then, I was asked if I had any tattoos. I answered, "No." They both gave a slight nod and continued with the questions. You could, in fact have tattoos and work in the middle east. There are lots of teachers there with tattoos. However, you can't show them while working or conducting school business. I thought the interview went well. If I didn't get the job, it wasn't because I didn't pass the interview. "It must not have been in God's plan," was my response to just about everything that didn't go my way.

The next morning, I woke up to an offer letter for an Academic Vice Principal position in my email. I was so excited because that was not the norm to receive an offer the next day to work abroad. Two weeks later, Deirdre found out she was hired as well. I was offered the position for 29,750 AED (Arab Emirate Dollars) a month plus I would receive a 5000 USD (United States Dollars) furniture allowance. The salary equated to about 8000 USD a month tax free. Which meant that I would make about 96K USD tax free, yearly. The contract was for employment for three years. The email stated in bold print "Do not quit your job right away." I'd heard that many times people quit their jobs too soon and would be left without a job due to a freeze on jobs or there would be some type of hold placed on the job offer.

My life was getting exhausting and I was so ready for a change in my life. I was so unhappy with life, my weight gain, my health, or how I looked at the world. I constantly thought to myself, "This can't be my life right now." I thought I had plans for my life, but really, I was just going through the motions of life. So, I eagerly signed my offer letter that morning and emailed it back to the recruiter and the process continued. I wanted my son and daughter to move with me. I told my ex-husband that I was moving to UAE to work for two years even though my contract was for three years. My recruiter said Abu Dhabi Education Council was only offering three-year contracts. They no longer offered two-year contracts, and I could get out of my contract after two years without any penalties.

Even though I signed the offer letter, I wasn't fully committed to moving. I prayed a lot about the move and even made statements like, "If Chelsea gets into the Atlanta Girls School, I'm not moving." "If my ex-husband doesn't let my daughter go, then I'm not moving." I knew my ex-husband would not allow my son to move out of the country. I wasn't going to fight him on that because I felt that my son needed his father. I felt a man could only teach a boy how to be a man.

My ex-husband was not on board however when I initially expressed that I was moving to the middle east as an administrator, he was not sure if he would allow Chelsea to move with me. He said, "That's too far and anything could happen. There is too much going on in the world." I expressed to Chelsea that I was moving and if she wanted to move with me, she had to work on getting her father to allow her to go. Chelsea was a mini version of me. If I wanted to do something, more than likely she wanted to do it, too. I was her role model and she made sure her teachers and everyone else knew it. Her teachers would always say, "Chelsea really looks up to you. She really admires her mother."

Chelsea was so hurt when her grandmother and uncle told her that she wasn't moving to the middle east. They told her that she could explore the United States and she didn't need a passport to do that. However, that didn't stop her from getting excited about moving. She told all her classmates and teachers that she was moving to Dubai. Her teachers were shocked when I confirmed that we were really moving to the United Arab Emirates.

I shared the move with my dad, family and friends. My dad was excited for me and wanted me to have the experience. One of his college friends had worked overseas and she really liked the experience. So, he wanted me to have the same good experience. When I told him that I might not go unless my ex-husband would allow Chelsea to go, he said, "Why should he dictate if you move or not?" He was right! I allowed my ex-husband to control so much of my life and it was time that I took control of my decisions.

With that said, I told my ex-husband that I was going to move to the middle east and he would have custody of both my son and daughter. I think I was still just talking. Deep down inside of me, I could not explore the world without my children. A month before I left for the United Arab Emirates, my ex-husband agreed to allow Chelsea to move with me and signed the letter of consent required by the education organization.

I knew that my son would not be allowed to go so I didn't push him on that. My son was only six years old and he really needed his father. He had been acting up a little in school. He was struggling to control his behavior and emotions. He was having a tough time dealing with the divorce. For instance, he would lash out and hit me and his sister when he didn't get his way. I felt increasingly sadden to leave him behind. I wanted all of us to go to counseling and made attempts to get us counseling services. However, between my schedule of trying to move and tie up loose ends and finding a reputable counselor, it didn't happen before I left. I continued to pray for my son's emotional well-being. He is the kind of kid that would give you so much love but would also be in a rage if he didn't get his way. I was going through so much emotional turmoil, but tried to maintain my normal mental state.

My heart was on an emotional rollercoaster. My son weighed heavy on my mind and heart. Prior to the move, I talked a lot about my son during my one-on-one counseling sessions that were few. I felt that my son was very mad about the break-up between his father and me. He had also witnessed his father and I become very disrespectful to one another, and I believe he thought he should do the same. I tried to have more genuine compassion for him. His behavior was so much like the little boys I worked with in the inner city who had a lot of anger built up and would lash out in the most violent and disrespectful way. A sticking point for me is that young black boys in the United States could feel the pressure of the world on them and didn't know how to handle the pressure and anxiety of the world attacking them. To move at a time when my son is facing the pressure of the world and the breakup of his parents was the toughest decision I've ever made. Many times, I thought about not going because maybe I was being selfish. However, I didn't want to miss out on an opportunity to find out my true purpose in life and the discovery of myself. This move was more than exploring the world and educating others. It was about exploring myself. Who was I? Who did I want to be? Who did God intend for me to be?

People go through the motions of life instead of living life with purpose. People yearn to discover their purpose in life. We live our lives based on how we were taught to live life. We're taught to get an education, start a career, get married, have a family, raise children, and then enjoy life. The enjoyment of life looks like whatever your environment said it should be like. Well by the time you do all these things, your years of living are limited. Especially, if you do life in that order. We never take the time to reflect on God's purpose or how our plans align with God's purpose and plan.

We misunderstand the verb, selflove. My dad always used the quote, "Only a poor frog doesn't protect his own pond." I now understood what that meant. This was an opportunity to protect and nourish my mind, body, and soul. What kind of mother would I be if I'm constantly miserable, depressed, and self-medicating with the wrong things? I may have looked good on the outside, but deep down inside I was in turmoil.

CHAPTER 3

THE WRITING ON THE WALL

The next day after signing my contract with Abu Dhabi Education Council, the Area Director of my school in Atlanta placed my principal and me on a bogus professional development plan (PDP). Some of the things that was expressed in the plan was not under my control as an Assistant Principal. The school was in one of the poorest areas in Atlanta. We faced many challenges that come along with working in the inner city. My principal and I had the exact same professional development plan, which really didn't make any sense. She was the principal, and I was the Assistant Principal, which had limited responsibilities and duties in comparison to the building administrator (aka the principal). Interestingly the things he had on the PDP were things we already had in place. This was our second year at one of the most impoverished schools in Atlanta. However, we had some growth after year one of being at the school.

As an administrator I wore many hats. I had to play the role of momma, counselor, therapist, psychiatrist, and more. The poverty mentality is real, meaning a lot of the poverty-stricken parents and students didn't genuinely feel like they could be extremely successful in school or life. I worked extremely hard and kept late hours working on changing the poverty mentality of the children and parents at the school, which was anything but easy. It was hard trying to let a child know that they could be whatever they wanted to be when they didn't believe it, or they are being told the opposite at home.

It was interesting how I was pouring into children but lacked the ability to pour into myself. The students came to school with dirty clothes, hungry, and lacked school supplies. I gave away a lot of my children's old clothes and shoes. The children were so thankful and appreciative. Our school gave away bookbags of food to the children sponsored by Hands on Atlanta every Friday. The kids looked forward to receiving the bags every week. They would drop the bookbags off in the front office on Monday and we would deliver the bookbags full of food to the classrooms on Friday. I loved what I did, but it was taking a toll on me emotionally. I had a relationship with the parents that was genuine and sincere. My relationship with the students was just as close.

For me, this mandated PDP was accusatory. It stipulated that I was not doing what was expected of me. I didn't appreciate the Area Director's lack of effectiveness. He never supported our school. The writing was on the wall and it was clear. The district did not want me or my principal to run the school just after being there two years. I think it was more about politics than performance. One month later, I was told by the area director that my principal and I had a chance to resign, because he was not going to recommend that we stay at the school the following year. I knew it was not fair. It was bogus and had absolutely no merit. I emailed the superintendent to see if she was aware of his recommendation and to see if she was in support of it. She stated that she could not comment on non-renewals because she makes the final decision; however, I did have tenure with the district and would be offered a teaching contract. I was not confident in her response. I could have fought the nonrenewal request, but I remembered my mother saying to me as a child, "Never stay where you are not wanted." So, I crafted my letter of resignation a week later.

The move to the middle east was becoming more and more real. I eventually made my announcement to the principal and my staff. They were all very supportive and wished me the best. The staff really like working with the principal and me, however, they knew more changes were forthcoming and many of them left the same year my principal and I left. Two of my teachers even announced they were also moving to teach in the middle east. The next school year, Atlanta Public Schools reconstituted the school I worked at and all the teachers and administrative staff were released of their teaching positions. If they wanted to work at the school, they had to reapply for their jobs. God has a way of moving you even if you think you are not ready.

Now that I made up in my mind that I was moving to the middle east, my life began moving at 100 mph and I had no time to breathe. Two weeks before I left, I received the email from my recruiter that I was moving ahead of time. I had to move out of my apartment because my lease was ending. I had to put all my things in storage, find a new owner for my dog Pepper, and find a moving company and reputable storage company to store all my things. I lived in my two-bedroom apartment for three years and it was really packed with stuff. I had over 200 pairs of shoes and every closet was filled. Shoe boxes were stacked in my room and in my storage room. I love shoes. I guess it was the only thing that remained constant—my shoe size. If it wasn't for my two best friends, I don't know how I would have been packed up and moved out in time before my lease ended. I didn't have a real boyfriend or male friend I felt comfortable enough to call for help.

The hassle of finding a home for my dog was even harder. My miniature Yorkie was 13 years old and was partly sick. She had seizures from time to time. However, she was very smart. My girlfriend's husband had a friend that knew a lady that would take Pepper. I should've taken more time to find a home for Pepper or just tried to bring her with me. However, it was too much of a hassle to get shots and all the necessary paperwork in just two weeks and do all the other things I had to do. I never met the lady and I wasn't even sure she went to a lady. I learned later that she was living in another state with the lady. I did receive a picture of Pepper laying on her dog blanket I sent with her. I really missed my dog. I pray for her all the time and I pray that we would be reunited one day. I would get so jealous when I saw people walking their dogs in the desert.

Next on my list was to make sure that I saw my dad before I moved. I bought a last-minute ticket to Detroit to see him. He was proud of me for deciding on my own and not allowing someone else to influence my decision to move. My father is a man that is highly respected, mild mannered in a cool way and leveled-headed always. I rarely heard my dad raise his voice. He and my mother were total opposites. As a young girl, my dad and I were very close. I'm his only biological daughter and I'm the oldest of his children. My dad's background was in counseling so talking to him was always easy. We still had our personal talks, but I felt like there were some things that he preferred that I experienced instead of him telling me the outcome.

Moving made way for my relationship with Chelsea to grow and flourish like no other. She and I talk about everything, although I don't talk to her like she's my girlfriend because I'm sure questions will come up that I'm not ready to answer. She was just as excited about the move as I was. We both wanted her brother Rylan to move with us, but I knew that wasn't possible as long as my ex-husband had the final say. The closer to my departure, the more mixed emotions I experienced. I was optimistic and felt guilty at the same time. A piece of my heart was being left behind.

CHAPTER 4

WELCOME TO ABU DHABI

Chelsea is my 11-year-old daughter who has a personality that is bigger than life at times. She reminds me so much of my mother. She never meets a stranger. She has been this way since birth. My mother would always tell me to stop Chelsea from just going up to strangers. She loves people! When she realized she was moving to Abu Dhabi with me, she was overly excited. She told just about everybody at school. She even told the people at Atlanta Girls School during her interview. All I could do was smile and shake my head when the lady said Chelsea told her during the interview she was moving to Dubai. I don't think she realized that she wasn't supposed to say that during the interview. I guess it wasn't God's will that she attends the Atlanta Girls School. However, I thought it would've been a good fit for her. God knows best. He knew that if she got into

Atlanta Girls School, I would've still been in Atlanta going through the motions of life. I had been praying for a more fulfilled life and this move was one of the ways God was answering my prayers.

When we arrived at Abu Dhabi International Airport, I wasn't impressed with the airport. I thought the airport would be more updated and on a grander scale. It was dingy with poor lighting. We had a total of four suitcases. Our life was now packed into four large suitcases. I had to pay three hundred dollars for the over the weight limit and the extra bags. We were greeted by someone holding the sign ADEC Teachers. There was a group of people that were arriving at the same time to work in the middle east. Our flight arrived in the evening and the sun was down. When we walked outside, we nearly suffocated from the overwhelming heat and high humidity. My glasses immediately fogged up. The heat and humidity were quite overbearing and made it hard to breathe initially. The first picture we took was Chelsea standing next to a camel statue. Chelsea had the biggest smile on her face. I knew I had to make things work for this little girl. She left all her friends, her brother, father, and swim team to move across the world to be with me, a black woman who was still trying to figure life out. I held her hand as we loaded on to a large charter bus with other educators and their families, while our bags were loaded underneath the bus. I don't remember seeing any other children Chelsea's age as much as I remember seeing a lot of married couples. We were driven to Novotel hotel in Abu Dhabi. According to my paperwork, I was supposed to go to a different hotel. As time went on, I learned that things can literally change at any moment with this country and school system. Depending on the mood of the Sheik, a holiday could be decreed, and we were all off work. I'm sure I'm overexaggerating, but it felt like that.

When we checked into the hotel, they asked for our passport and we were given a room key. I didn't see my passport again until about month later. Novotel was our home for the next five days. During those five days, I learned how to order take out from my cell phone using an app called Talabot and have it delivered to the hotel. Talabot became our best friend for the next five months.

All the teachers and administrators had a few orientation meetings. One of the meetings was about our new culture. During the meeting, we learned that women should never show the soles of their shoes. Men should only shake the hand of a Muslim woman when she extends her hand first. We were told that Abu Dhabi translates to "place rich in Arabian gazelle." An Arabic proverb, "Eat what you like, dress for others." Which leads me to dress. We were told women are expected to cover their legs to their ankle and their arms to below the elbows. If a woman wears pants, she should wear a top that covers her buttocks. In addition to learning about the dress code, we were all preparing to become residents of the United Arab Emirates.

The process of gaining our residential visa required a medical exam. We were loaded onto large charter buses and taken to a center to apply for our Emirates Id and complete a medical exam. The medical exam included an AIDS/HIV test, Hepatitis B, Leprosy, Pregnancy, Syphilis, Tuberculosis (TB), and chest x-ray. During the medical exam, we were extremely quiet. You could tell we were a little unsure of the tests result even after the exam. The process to obtain a visa was new to me. It made me think about the processes in the United States. Two days later we were all loading a bus again headed to our assigned regions. This was an indication that the test results were fine. I heard that some people were sent home. People think it was due to the test results. I heard that people are sent back home every year due to test results. I can't imagine what it would be like to pack up your whole life and move to a foreign country to learn that you have a serious illness and can't enter.

While Chelsea and I were in Abu Dhabi city, we went on a big bus tour in which we learned quite a bit about the UAE. We learned that the country was only 45 years old at the time we were there. I had to remind myself of the country's age through the trials and tribulations of navigating new lands. The country conducted business with no sense of urgency or efficiency. The country was founded in 1971, with Sheikh Zayed bin Sultan Al Nahyan as its first president. Everywhere we went there were pictures of him, the current president of UAE, and the Sheikh of Abu Dhabi. The population of UAE is made up of 85 percent expatriates and 15 percent local Emirates. In addition, the tour guide talked about how the Arabs were convinced to dig for oil by the British and go along with the styles of the Arabic men and women. The women wear black Abayas with a Shayla while the men wear white Kanduras. To demonstrate their style, the women display their style by dressing the abayas up with fancy jewelry on the back, sequins, and jewels, accessorized with fashionable handbags, shoes, and fancy henna tattoos on their hands and arms.

The United Arab Emirates is like no other country I've ever experienced. I learned that the women that are from the Emirates wear black Abayas and Shaylas and the women from other countries wear other color abayas. The country was over saturated with white colored cars. I had never seen so many white colored cars in my life. I was told that the people of UAE loved white, for it is the color of purity. I'm still wondering how in the world they kept the Kanduras so white. I saw a few dingy ones, but not very many. Our first experience to UAE left Chelsea and I wanting to learn more, and really find out more about the Emiratis. Our nerves slightly eased as we embarked on our new home in Al Ain, Abu Dhabi.

CHAPTER 5

WELCOME TO AL AIN REGION

Al Ain is the region where I was assigned to live and work. It is located between Dubai and Abu Dhabi. From Al Ain, it takes about 1 hour and 45 minutes to get to Abu Dhabi and about 1 hour and 15 minutes to get to Dubai by car. The Danat hotel was our home for the next two weeks as we looked for a place of our own. Novotel was a lot nicer than the Danat. The Danat had two nice pools. Al Ain had large malls just like Abu Dhabi. I've never experienced so many huge malls in my life. The best malls were in Dubai and Abu Dhabi. Every mall had a place just for kids. Chelsea loved the kid's places. They are a mixture of Six Flags, Chuck E. Cheese, and Dave & Busters. There is always something here for children to do.

Most, if not all the Emirati families, had a nanny for their children. It was so strange for us to see families in the mall with the nanny following behind the children in tow. There were nannies from all over the world, though they were generally from Ethiopia and the Philippines. Most of the nannies kept their hair covered in a Shayla or Hijab. I heard a family could get a live-in nanny for as little as 1000 AED a month which is about $272 USD a month. Now I see why so many families had a nanny. The benefit outweighed the cost.

After moving to Al Ain, I had about two weeks to find a place to live and move in. It really wasn't as difficult as it was for some people. I heard about a villa community that would be perfect for me. I went with two other young ladies to look at the property. Al Oyoun Village was perfect for Chelsea and me. Our place had three bedrooms, two and a half baths, and a maid's quarter with another bathroom. I didn't hire a live-in maid, but I did have someone clean the house biweekly. We had a closed-in backyard with a nice patio. The living room had an open floor plan that reminded us of home. The walls were made of cement which required a power drill to hang pictures. The cement walls muffled the sound of the Adhan, or prayer call that was required six times a day. I usually got the maintenance men to hang pictures. All the floors were made of ceramic tile including the stairs and all the bedrooms. Each room had its own thermostat control. I learned after a few weeks that the air doesn't automatically turn off after it reaches a certain temperature. You must manually turn it off. There was no window treatment, refrigerator, stove, washer, or dryer. I wasn't accustomed to renting a place that didn't have window treatment, or even a stove. However, I was so excited about getting out of the hotel that I overlooked what was missing. I could finally cook a regular meal. I could tell that eating out every day was taking its toll on my waistline. My clothes were starting to feel tight. The villa complex had a community swimming pool, gym, tennis court and playground for kids. The neighborhood was a blend of families from all over the world. Each family had a two-car parking driveway.

Al Ain is a lot more traditional than Abu Dhabi and Dubai. There were a lot of more local people living there. The malls were full of Muslims wearing abayas and kanduras. Many of the women were fully covered including their face, hands, and feet. I asked several Muslim women why the women covered up in that manner. I was given several answers. One Muslim woman from Jordan said it's because the husband wants his wife to cover her face so other men won't see her face and be tempted. I wondered if they realize that lust begins in the heart. Another Muslim local woman said it was done out of tradition. However, I was also told that depends on the woman's family upbringing. If you were raised to cover your face completely, then would continue to cover it even after marriage. It really irritated me to see a woman cover her face in public because it seems as if she doesn't want people to know that she exists in the world. All the bus monitors on my job all covered completely. I can only assume they don't want the bus driver or any other men to be tempted in some way. Adapting to the culture was difficult and very hard to adjust.

Aside from the legalistic clothing, there are physical differences, too. For example, women and men are completely separated. There is a separate waiting area for women at the hospitals, post offices, and even at the local place to pay your power bill. Never did I witness seeing Muslim women and men in UAE mix and mingle at a social gathering - including their weddings!

Buying Furniture

Buying furniture was a process that became tiresome really fast. My new friend who just moved from Houston, Texas and I visited a gentleman's house that was known for selling used furniture. We were overwhelmingly surprised to see all the stuff the man was selling. He had furniture literally everywhere! When we entered the gate, there were two makeshift sheds with all kinds of refrigerators, stoves, beds, tables, televisions and more. The furniture was full of dust and sand. It was hard to really look and get around the shed because there was furniture in every nook and cranny. Then his cat would run by you or stare at you like you were invading his space. After looking at the furniture, my friend decided to buy a table. She had to make a deposit, so he invited us into his house where his wife and children were. I couldn't believe my eyes. It was more clutter of stuff that belonged to him and to sell. The wife was in the kitchen that was full of all kinds of household items which looked stuffed in every nook and corner. We sat on the edge of a sofa to write down the details of the sale. I was too afraid to sit back on the sofa. I thought a bug might jump on me. We could see two children playing in a room that was stuffed to capacity of a bunkbed, dressers, boxes, and more. The house was completely covered in junk. On top of everything else, his house smelled like an old basement full of old furniture and greasy food. We couldn't wait to get out of there. We had just experienced bargaining with a real live hoarder. They were hoarders! My friend even tried to buy a small television that was clearly not being used in the house, but they refused to sell it. We laughed about how this Muslim family could very well be on the American show, *Hoarders*.

Since our townhouse also referred to as a flat, needed so many things, we had a lot of shopping to do. I was so shocked that our townhome didn't have any window treatment or appliances. It was very different then moving into an apartment in the United States. The furniture was priced a lot cheaper than what I was accustomed to seeing in the states. For example, a three-piece custom-made living room set cost about 3000 Dirhams which is about 800 USD. The appliances were equally inexpensive. However, the quality of the appliances was not good. Three different friends had the glass on their stove to shatter while they were in middle of cooking. Also, my refrigerator's freezer stopped working. I guess you get what you pay for. I had a Daewoo stove and refrigerator. I didn't know Daewoo made appliances. Daewoo was one of the few brands that I recognized. A lot of the brands were not American brands we were accustomed to seeing. There were Italian and Turkish brands the sales associate would try to sell us. One of the things I kept noticing was the locks on the refrigerators. I asked the associate, "Why are there locks on the refrigerators?"

"To keep the children out," he said.

"Do you see how these kids behave?" Deirdre whispered as we shopped for appliances.

"Do you think the parents keep them from getting food?" I asked the sales associate.

"Those locks are there to keep the kids from getting the food."

"Why won't the parents just pop the kid's hand?" I asked the sales associate.

He laughed and dragged out, "No, you can't do that. Spanking children in UAE is frowned upon."

There were websites like Dubizzle that allowed people to buy and sell furniture, cars, real estate, and more. Also, there were Facebook groups for people selling items in the area. Most people bought from the local furniture stores, which weren't exactly many in number. So more than likely multiple people had the same furniture, but maybe in different colors. It took me a while to pick out furniture. I wanted to get something that I was going to be okay with for the next three years.

The first thing I bought was my appliances. I bought a stainless-steel Daewoo stove and refrigerator. The stove was a gas stove that required a gas cylinder. I had to go to the gas station to buy a gas cylinder and then I had to purchase a hose that stretched long enough from the cylinder which was outside the house in a storage box through a hole that led inside my villa and then connected to the stove. The first hose I bought wasn't long enough. I paid one of the maintenance men 20 AED to connect everything together. I was too afraid of blowing up something. In order to use the stove, I had to turn the knob and press the ignition button. The process reminded me so much of my childhood when my mom would have to light the oven part of the stove with a match. It took me a minute to learn how to use my own stove because I was afraid of blowing up something.

Trying to convert my villa into a home took a while, but it was decent. I finally bought some furniture at the last minute which turned out to be nothing like I expected. I expected to get some comfy Lazy Boy style furniture. I bought a custom-made couch, chair, and loveseat. The cushions were so hard you would break a bone trying to plop on it. It wasn't the kind of couch you could easily fall asleep on either. I was so upset, but I dealt with it. We were getting tired of sitting at the dining room table to watch tv. We wanted to relax. Plus, I never paid for the rest of it. In fact, when I told the salesmen that I wanted to get different cushions due to the hardness, he never called me back about the rest of the money I owed him for the living room set. Spending time furniture shopping was what I did for the first couple of months once I moved into my villa. It took a while to get all the furniture and appliances I needed. I finally did, but getting the furniture was just the first step in my journey settling in.

Our first special day in the UAE was Chelsea's birthday. We had been in the UAE only eleven days and were still living in a hotel. We had no real transportation of our own, so we caught a taxis to get around Al Ain. I wanted her birthday to be special. Chelsea was a social butterfly and had made friends with people in the hotel before I did. Everybody knew Chelsea. This was her eleventh birthday, and she was a thousand miles away from our family and friends. We had been in the country for eleven days and I only knew two other people who stayed at the same hotel, Deirdre and Tasha. However, I quickly made friends with a couple other young ladies, Tiffany and Meron, who later became my neighbors. Meron was the only one who had rented a car. She and Tiffany were sharing a rental car while we were staying in the hotel. As I said, I really wanted Chelsea's birthday to be special, but it was quite difficult since I didn't know where any of the grocery stores were nor did I have access to Walmart because there weren't any there. The way the government is set up, they will probably never have a Walmart. I didn't even have a car to get around. I didn't know where we were moving. I was on the hunt to find a place for us to live. I had told Chelsea that I would get her a cake and invite some of the other kids staying at the hotel to have cake with us. Well the entire day was spent running around to different rental properties and home stores, which prevented me from getting my baby girl a birthday cake. Inside I felt horrible and wanted to cry because this was the first year I hadn't bought my daughter a birthday cake or anything. She didn't seem upset. She played in the stores and helped pick out appliances and home décor. She was definitely a kid that didn't demand much if anything at all. I think she looked at the experience of moving and exploring a new country as a treat. She ended up playing cards with two little girls that were vacationing from Germany. She was content as she showed the girls how to play card games like Concentration and Speed. Knowing that she was unbothered and content to be in the company of other kids made me feel a little better.

As parents we want to give our children so much, not realizing that quality time is the most effective and beneficial for them. Learning more about Chelsea and learning how quality time and conversations had an impact on her development was becoming more meaningful.

Traffic and Transportation

When we arrived in UAE, we were introduced to several rental car places. At the time of our arrival and settling in, renting a car was our only reasonable mode of transportation. Thrifty and National car rentals were the two main companies. The price to rent a vehicle for a month in UAE was a lot cheaper than renting a vehicle for the month in the United States. My four-door white Nissan Sunny with manual window handles in the rear cost about 1200 AED which equals about $326 USD. Did I mention I converted everything, and I mean literally *everything*? If it was not a reasonable U.S. price, then I did not buy it. For example, there was sparkling water imported from the United States that cost $20 USD. I refused to pay that much for a 12 pack of sparkling water. However, most things I purchased were reasonable. It was very reasonable and convenient to get your car washed.

So, one day a man stopped by my villa and offered to wash my car two days a week for 150 AED a month. When I did the conversion, that was $5 USD per wash. I definitely jumped at that deal. Especially, since I did not have to leave my home. I hated going to the carwash, and it was nice to have my car cleaned while sleeping. I would wake up to a sparkling white car with the windshield wipers lifted indicating that my car had been washed. I thought that was one of my best and favorite deals while living in the UAE.

Many of my colleagues had drivers that would drop them off at school and sit patiently waiting for them to walk out at 1:45 pm each day. The cost of a driver was about the same as the cost of a nanny. A driver could cost you about 1000-1500 AED, which was again between $272-400 USD. I was tempted at times to hire a driver. I had only been in UAE for 10 months and had already been in two car accidents and received well over 10 traffic violations. Whereas in the United States I had been in two accidents and maybe received four traffic violations my entire driving career. I would joke with my friends that Al Ain streets were full of squares and circles. There was no way you could get lost in this town. The circles consisted of roundabouts. There were many roundabouts in the city. The roundabouts took the place of a four-way traffic light. There were four ways to enter the roundabout, and, once in it, you had to pray to get out of it. There could be cars entering and exiting the roundabout at different types of speeds. There have been many accidents approaching the rounding and within the roundabout.

My first car accident was approaching a roundabout. There was one car in front of me that was at the roundabout. There were no cars coming from my left and I expected the car in front of me to enter the roundabout and go. So, I pressed on the gas and ran directly into the back of the car in front of me. I was so upset. I couldn't understand why she didn't just go. However, she stated that she couldn't see past the car next to her which made a lot of since. There are usually two to three lanes of cars trying to approach the roundabout on the same side you are approaching the roundabout. So, imagine three lanes of traffic approaching a circle with three lanes of traffic in four different directions. Yeah, it's a scary feeling initially. If you don't move fast enough someone will blow their horn. This city blows their horns more than the taxi drivers in New York City. It's so annoying too, especially when they blow their horn as soon as a traffic light turns green.

Driving in the fog is even worse. The fog in the desert is like no other fog I've ever seen in my life. You can barely see your hand in front of your face when the fog is very thick. School was delayed several times due to the thickness of the fog. I remember driving in the heavy fog for the first time. I was driving to work, and I had just dropped Chelsea off at school. It was clear when I drove her to school. However, as

I began to make my way to the main highway, the fog became more and more dense. Therefore, I slowed down a lot and turned on my windshield wipers to get rid of some of the precipitation. That did not work at all. It was like a thick cloud had swallowed my car. Meanwhile, there were cars creeping behind me, zooming on the side of me, and inching around the roundabouts in front of me. I was so nervous that I turned on my hazard lights to indicate I'm not moving any faster. Because of the fog, I missed my turn onto the main highway and made a wrong turn. Because I knew my way to work, I didn't use a GPS.

The sidewalks slowly disappeared and became sand dunes. I was wondering where my turn was because I didn't recall passing sand dunes this close to my car. Then it dawned on me—I was in the wrong area. The road was no longer paved. It had turned into gravel, rocks, and sand. On either side of the road were sheds that looked like they were made from tin with barbed wire around them. There were a few animals that looked like llamas, but I couldn't tell because the fog was still so thick. I was scared to death. I had no idea where I was or if I was on private property. All I could think about was being abducted in the middle of nowhere and Trump not trying to save me. A few men riding camels quickly passed me on a camel track. I begin to pray. "God, please help me get out of here. I need your help, Lord. In the name of Jesus, don't let my car detonate a bomb in this desert,

Lord. In the name of Jesus, Amen." I grabbed my cell phone and pulled up the maps app and quickly hit work which was saved on the app. Thankfully, the internet service worked well enough to help me navigate through some of the roughest parts I'd ever seen in the desert to the main highway and then on to work. I learned from that date forward that if the fog is thick just pull over to the side of the road and wait. A couple of days later, there was a 30-40 car pile-up in Abu Dhabi due to fog and people driving like it was a normal speeding day. The locals drove as though they were invincible. I saw more accidents there in one year than I have seen in my whole life in the United States.

Also, I've seen people drive extremely recklessly. Chelsea, one of my friends, and I were leaving Chelsea's school play on a Thursday night. The traffic was bumper to bumper. It was the beginning of the weekend and more cars were on the road. A gentleman behind me decided to blow his horn at me because I allowed a truck to get in front of me. The truck was turning in front of me from another street. The traffic was moving slowly, so it was no big deal to allow the driver to get in front of me. When the traffic started to pick up more, the truck behind me sped up on the side of me bogarting his way to get in front of me. He almost caused me to hit the truck in front of me, and he almost hit the truck in front of him. I leaned on my horn at him. I was so pissed and couldn't believe he would do such a stupid thing while there is so much traffic on the road. I looked at his tinted window and yelled, "What the fuck are you doing?" He rolled his window down, and I yelled again, "What the fuck are you doing?"

He placed his finger to his tongue and said, "Watch your tongue."

Then I said to him again, "What are you doing?" "You could've killed us!"

The man spoke in a matter-of-fact tone, "You not in London, or USA. I know how to drive."

I yelled, "But you don't know if I know how to drive and you could've killed us." The traffic began to move, and I allowed the man to get in front of me. My girlfriend reminded me that profanity was not allowed in the country and just to let the man go. The man could have reported me to the police department for cursing, and I could've been arrested. No witness or proof is needed to corroborate the accusation for a person to be arrested.

There have been several incidents where people have flipped the bird at a local Emirati and were arrested and put in jail. Sometimes when driving, other drivers will speed up behind you and flash their lights. That is an indication for you to move over a lane and allow them to pass by. That usually happened when a person drove in the far-left lane. I was told that one day a doctor was driving in the middle lane and a car behind him flashed his lights at him wanting him to pull over into the far-right lane. However, the doctor did not get into the far-right lane. The next day, the doctor received a letter stating that he needed to apologize to a Sheik for not getting into the next lane or he needed to leave the country. In the end, the UAE had one less doctor. You must be careful when driving. It is best to know the traffic laws and the laws of the country. I really wished they went over the traffic laws and all the speed trapping cameras during orientation.

The wind in the desert can be just as dangerous as the fog. The mixture of the wind and sand is so fierce at times that it can blow your car from one lane into the next. No one ever taught me how to drive in a sandstorm. One day I was driving home from work while the force of the wind rocked my little Nissan Sunny from side to side. I did not know what to do. The sand was so thick that I had to turn on my windshield wipers to see the road. Meanwhile, the road bullies in the Pathfinders and Pilots were zooming by me. I slowed down until the wind gave way and then I would pick up speed. I wondered if the speed trap cameras would add speed to my car with the wind. I had enough tickets to last me a lifetime. I nervously drove slowly against the tornado-like wind and sand mixture until I safely arrived at my destination.

Because we lived in a desert with heavy winds, there would always be sand everywhere in my townhome during a wind storm. The sand found its way under my front door and into my living and dining room, under my kitchen window and all over my kitchen sink. I was not an expert at cleaning sand and had never experienced sand all in my house or my apartment in the states. So, I called our cleaning lady from the Philippines, which is the origin country of most of the housekeepers and nannies in UAE. It was quite remarkable how she would vacuum and complete submerge our ceramic tiled floors with water to get rid of the sand. Driving and battling the sand and wind in the desert was an experience that I will always remember.

Work Assignment

I was assigned by the school system to work at an all Kindergarten (KG) school outside of Al Ain. The school educates children that are between the ages of four and five. These same children would be considered pre-kindergarten and kindergarten students in the United States. It is considered a desert school because of the forty or more miles outside Al Ain and Abu Dhabi. A small community of homes only surrounded the school. No major stores or buildings were near. It took me about 50 minutes to drive to work. On my way to work, I passed lots of camels and sand dunes and plenty of speed trap cameras. The long drive gave me lots of time to think and meditate about my life and what in the world I was doing in the middle east.

My school was staffed with all women. Most of the teachers were not from the United Arab Emirates. However, the office staff were from UAE. There were five teachers that were English Speaking Teachers and Eight were Arab Speaking Teachers. Most of the women wore a black Abaya with a Shayla. Most of the time you can see a colorful Jalabiya peeking underneath. One day my principal and I were sitting in her office on the nice black leather couch. I noticed she kept looking down at my skirt. The skirt was slightly above my ankle. I had a pair of wedge sandals to compliment the ensemble. After the conversation, as I was leaving, my principal said to me in her Arabic accent, "Ms. Theresa, don't take this the wrong way, but your skirt must come down to your ankle. It's ADEK policy." I said, "Thank you, and I will fix it." That weekend, I bought two black Abayas. I wore an Abaya without the Shayla to work every day.

The two Abayas I purchased had snaps in the front, so you could just snap them open or closed. However, they were exceptionally long. They were long enough that when I sat down and crossed my legs the Abaya would still cover my ankle. I felt like I could wear anything under my Abaya, so I thought. One day I decided to wear my cute little orange dress underneath. As I turned, my principal could see my bare leg through the snaps of my Abaya. Her eyes got extremely wide. and she said my name in such a way that it startled me.

"Theresa, I can see your leg when you turn! You VP! You must set the example!"

I thought to myself, "Damn it!" I knew I had to get these darn things sewn closed, so people have no idea what I have underneath. I purchased two more Abayas that were completely closed so now I could wear anything underneath and no one could see through it. I wore workout clothes under my Abaya just about every day with a pair of flipflops. Dressing up for work like I did in the United States was a thing of the past. I proudly rocked an Abaya to work every day and when I arrived home, it was the first thing I took off.

The security guard was the only male staff on the school campus. He was our 24-hour security that lived in a guard house right outside the school. Both the school and the guard house were surrounded by a brick fence. We had one security guard that was from the Philippines and one from Africa. They took turns working shifts. All the women on my staff were Muslim except four expat teachers and myself. Everyone else spoke and understood Arabic fluently. Therefore, all the staff meetings led by the principal, or another staff member were conducted in Arabic and translated in English. I felt like when it was translated, it was a shorten version of what was really said. The students were taught core classes such as reading and math in English by the English-speaking teachers. The students were learning to speak English at a very early age. This was the case in all the government schools. The country wanted the children to learn to speak English fluently.

All the children native language was Arabic, so the morning assembly was mainly conducted in Arabic with no translation. All the students were transported by the public-school bus. Sometimes a child walked to school accompanied by their nanny if they missed the school bus. The school buses begin dropping students off at 7:45 am and they were dismissed at 12:30 pm. I was amazed about the hours at the beginning of the school year. The first week of school, students were dismissed at 10:00 am and the second week 11:00am and by the third week they left at the regularly scheduled time of 12:30 pm. The students are taught English Literacy, Math, and Science in the English language from and English speaking teachers. Their other courses such as Art, Islamic Education, Arabic Literacy, are taught in the Arabic Language. This may explain why a lot of the Muslim people in UAE spoke English fluently enough to carry on a conversation and a relationship with an English-speaking person. This is much different than other countries I have visited. Speaking English in other countries such as Thailand made the person more employable. Most of my Arabic staff admitted to learning English in school and through American music. My school's population was right under 140 students. A school that size in the United States would be on its way to closing due to the lack of children.

There was a separate parking lot for the administration and the teachers. Once we enter through the gate to park our cars, the security guard closes the gates, and they remain closed until we exit the school grounds at the end of the day. I wondered if the elementary schools in the United States had 24-hour security would that prevent some of the school break-ins and vandalism, that occurs at some schools. Since I've been here, I haven't heard of anyone breaking into the schools, teachers' cars being stolen, or kids vandalizing the property. In addition to the 24-hour security guards, the school still has cameras everywhere. There are no blind spots in the school except in the classroom. Meaning, there is a camera that can see every inch of the building.

I've always thought about putting cameras in the classrooms like they do at some of the daycare centers. I've always wondered if this would curtail some of the misbehaviors of students and teachers in the classroom. When people know that they are being watched, their behaviors tend to change. It appeared to be cameras everywhere in the United Arab Emirates. If you commit a crime in public, a camera in this country will surely catch it on camera! There was little crime in Abu Dhabi, but when there was, a camera helped solve the crime.

There was a case where three young Arabic men abducted a Asian woman and drove her to the desert and took turns raping her and then dropped her back off near the location where she was abducted. They were all arrested because the cameras on the street were able to identify the three boys and the vehicle they were driving. The case is currently pending trial. Another case involved an eight-year-old boy who was lured to a rooftop by a man dressed in an Abaya. The boy was sexually assaulted and murdered by a Pakistani man. Once again, cameras were able to capture the assailant luring the kid and helped solve the case. The man was ordered to death by execution. There is no such thing as an appeal in a case like this.

My school was not short of support personnel. There was a full-time nurse who we did not have to share with other area schools. The schools in Abu Dhabi didn't share a school nurse like it is done in some of the schools in the United States. However, some schools in the U.S. have a full-time school nurse or they have no nurse at all. In the UAE, my school transported kids on three school buses. Each bus had a full-time bus monitor who rode the bus with the kids every day. During the school hours, the bus monitors supported the school by making sure parents signed into the school properly. They supported lunch by monitoring students and helping them with their lunch in the cafeteria. The ladies only spoke Arabic and knew little English. However, they would always greet me in English, "Hello, Ms. Theresa." They had such a mild demeanor and were so patient with the children.

One of the ladies gifted me with the prettiest Abaya. It has such beautiful pleats that made me feel like a princess.

School celebrations were truly aligned with the Arabic culture, which included all cultures that are part of the Arabic descent. However, Emirati culture is unique. By the way, when I use the term Arabic, I'm referring to Egyptians, Jordanians, Pakistani, Palestinian, and other Arab countries. You may say I'm crazy for lumping them together, but that's the way I see it and have experienced it. Anyway, a celebration can involve anything that you have accomplished. While in school, we had a couple of accomplishments. We celebrated the birth of two of our staff members babies, a teacher earning the Khalifa Award, teachers earning their master's degree, and many more. One of the celebrations involved everyone sitting on a large decorated carpet, with legs crisscrossed and feet bare. Food was in the center. Some of the ladies ate with a spoon and fork and some ate with their hands. Yes, this culture like many other cultures eat with their hands. I personally didn't feel comfortable eating with my hands, so I ate with a fork. The food normally consisted of rice, chicken, salad, lots of bread, sauces, veggies, and delicious desserts that weren't too sweet. I learned that my new expat friends also experienced celebrations at their school. As a result, many of them gained weight "going to the carpet" as we called it. The Arabic teachers would often say to the English speaking teachers, "Come to the carpet." I was not a big fan of Arabic food, and I didn't eat much of it.

It was obvious the Emiratis were a fan of their own food, just like I was a fan of American food. I remember, I baked a Duncan Hines chocolate cake for the staff for Happiness Day. Finding American food products was rare, so Chelsea and I got really excited when we came across familiar food products. The two American teachers loved it! One said, "It made me feel like I was at home in the U.S." Another teacher said, "Thank you so much! It reminded me of my mom's cake." The Arabic teachers didn't say a word until I asked, and then they only said, "Thank you for the cake." I understood how they felt which was the exact same feeling I had about Arabic food.

The school was a warm environment, but it was obvious that the teachers feared the principal, Ms. Aisha. She had been the principal for several years and was very stern with the teachers and had high expectations. The women all got along very well and supported each other. My school slowly started to feel like a family. However, there were many times I felt a little confuse due to the language barrier which made me question my purpose. I engaged in consistent self-reflection on the job. Ms. Hasna, an Emirati teacher who was more like an instructional coach helped me navigate the school culture as much as possible. She was very fluent with English in reading, writing, and speaking. My transition into the school was frustrating at times because of the unclear expectations which was in part due to the language.

Teacher Evaluation

Part of my job as a school administrator was to conduct teacher evaluations. The final teacher evaluation system was based on a rubric with scores of 1through 5 in different categories, with five being the highest score. The teachers would debate the principal and me about their evaluation if they received less than a five. They felt like they should've had a perfect score. Even after asking for their evidence which they lacked, they still wanted a perfect score. I even asked a teacher, "What do you want?" She responded, "All five." The Muslim teachers would have a serious attitude if they didn't get a perfect score. I heard the same stories about teachers rebutting their evaluations at my principal friends' school.

I understood their griping. The evaluation rubrics were in English and Arabic. The wording and statements were not the exact same which made it very difficult to evaluate. For example, in English the wording would say "meets with parents," and in Arabic for the same score it would say, "Keeps communication record with parents." It would be incumbent of the principals to decide. The system really needed to throw away the whole teacher evaluation system and start all over. Throughout the school year, a totally different evaluation was conducted that wasn't like the final evaluation system. During the school year, when teachers were evaluated, the principal only had to write three strengths and three areas of growth about the teacher's practice. Subsequently, we administrators had to ensure that what we said throughout the school year matched what we were saying on the final evaluation. That was a major challenge and very subjective.

Some of the same students and grading issues aroused at the schools in Abu Dhabi as they did in the United States. Many of the teachers that were from the United States stated that the grades they put into the system for students were changed without their knowledge or approval. Students went from failing grades to passing grades. It was rumored in the UAE that if teachers spoke up about grade changes, then they would be transferred from the school or even terminated for no apparent reason. I don't believe students grades should be altered or changed. This gave students a false sense of achievement, and teachers just didn't say anything to administration. I was told by a teacher that parents have tried to come to school and take the tests for students on the computer. High school American teachers that were now in UAE teaching complained that some of the students devalued education. The same sentiments were felt in the United States. Students that scored below 80 could retake tests and redo projects. Emirati students took their Islamic courses a lot more seriously than the courses that were taught in

English. The classes taught in English were math, English Language Arts, and Science. My teacher and administrator friends shared so many stories about students' lack of motivation for school. For instance, a boy answered his phone in the middle of a test to finish a deal about selling a falcon for one million dirhams. The teenage boy refused to end the call or step outside to finish it. Middle school were the most disrespectful to the school property and adults. The girls outnumbered the boys when it came to attending college. The ratio of boys to girls at the local university was 1 to 20. The boys just didn't attend the local university as much as the girls. Instead, most went on to the military, studied abroad, or got a job. The girls that didn't go to college right away married very young to older men in their family.

The family of the girls did not allow them to study abroad like they did for the boys. Also, I don't think the government would pay for the girls to study abroad alone. One of my staff members was working on her master's degree at the local university. She explained that she wanted to attend college in the United States, but her parents would not allow her. She was a very charismatic and motivated educator. She was very passionate about education and would make a good administrator one day. I felt bad for her because she wanted to achieve more but was stifled by her family and the government.

I found the schools varied depending on where you were. The schools that were located further away from the city had parents that were a lot more laidback. However, in the city the students and parents seemed to be more aggressive. There were more behavior issues in the city. A friend that teaches at a girls' middle school showed me pictures of the students tearing up the classrooms for no reason. She said that a student pushed her. The school did not suspend the student. There was a parent teacher conference that was conducted all in Arabic. As a result, the student only apologized to the teacher. However, there was no major consequence for the student. This is very similar to what happens at the boys' school. There are no major consequences for students who were disrespectful.

An expat teacher shared that one student kept telling the teacher to "eat dog shit" in Arabic. The teacher was an English-speaking teacher and didn't understand what the student was saying until an administrator walked by and heard the student. He told the teacher what the student was saying and scolded the student verbally. However, there was nothing done to the student outside of the verbal scolding.

Students that may have only had one Emirati parent and their other parent was from another country were not offered advancements. For example, students that scored high on an exam were invited to a meeting for advance placement courses. Students that scored high that only had an Emirati father were excluded from the invitation. When English teachers inquired about why certain students weren't invited, they were told it was for students that had Emirati mothers and fathers. It was very common for Emirati men to marry a Filipino or Indian woman as their second, third, or even their fourth wife. The women could not apply for Emirati citizenship until after seven years of being married to the Emirati man. There were a lot of benefits to Emirati citizenship in the United Arab Emirates. Women that were from countries that didn't have as many privileges were willing to be a second or third wife to an Emirati.

My principal and I had many personal conversations about family, religion, and kids. She and I talked about the differences between what was in the Quran and what was in the Bible. I remember her saying in her Arabic accent, "Ms. Theresa, why you not read the Quran?" "You can translate," she said.

Not to offend her, I just said, "I don't know." The truth was, I never read the Quran because I've never had a desire or interest in reading it. My upbringing never exposed me to the Quran. She and I compared the stories in the Bible and the Quran. Many people may not know that Jesus appears in the Quran. I was amazed and intrigued how the two books shared similarities. It was like comparing a movie to the book version.

She used her phone to show me pictures and video of when she visited the cathedrals in Italy. She was in amazement of the beauty of the cathedrals and how they asked people to cover their head upon entering one of them.

"See, Ms. Theresa they cover they head in the what you call it?"

"Cathedral," I said.

She had a smile that basically said we, as in Muslims were are right in covering our heads. I responded back with a smile. I then added, "We cover our head in church as an usher during communion." That was not completely true, I've only seen it done at the older churches. It was like we both were proud of our religion and wanted to let the other person know that there were traditions that took place.

My principal was very passionate and proud to be an Emirati. Our conversations would at times focus on how she and the country loved Sheik Zayed. She shared a story about a man that had a large rug of Sheik Zayed in his store and a Pakistani wanted to purchase the rug. He offered the man two to three hundred thousand AED to purchase the rug. However, the store owner still refused to sell it. He even videotaped the man turning down the large amounts of money to sell the rug. As a result, one of the current sheiks went to the man's store to thank him for not selling the rug. I think he didn't sell it because he just didn't want the

Pakistani to own the rug with the Sheik on it. My principal shared that story to let me know how much respect and love the people of UAE had for Sheik Zayed.

One of my favorite staff members was a 26-year-old Muslim girl who was in love with Snapchat. She and I would have girl talk conversations from time to time. She was married to her first cousin. Her mother and her husband's mother were sisters. She was really into make-up and beauty products. She loved to see the different braided hairstyles, so she could post them on her Snapchat account. She loved to put the English teachers on Snapchat with the cute little filters. "Come, Ms. Theresa. "Can I take picture? "Can I post on Snapchat?" she would ask.

"Sure," I would respond. I didn't mind taking pictures and being on her Snapchat. Then she would hold up her iPhone to take my picture or make a video. She was such a beautiful person on the inside and out.

"Can I take your picture?" I asked.

"Only for your eyes," she said.

"I will only share it with my sisters in America." I would tell her. She would then take the picture with her face covered, only showing her eyes.

I didn't understand the purpose of taking a picture with only the eyes shown. That was the norm for the women to cover their face when taking a picture at work. Most would cover their face completely not even showing their eyes. Can you imagine looking at a picture with four women with only their eyes shown dressed in all black? I thought it was weird for the ladies to take a picture with students for award ceremonies and not show their face. If you're not going to show your eyes or face, why get in the picture? I thought the picture of me and several other teachers with their face completely covered looked silly. How would I know who was who if their entire faces were covered? It would have been better if they just didn't take the picture.

What was even more interesting was that they all had snapchat accounts where they posted pictures of themselves in their regular clothes with nothing on their hair. I wondered if this was a way to show other women how beautiful they were, so they could get hooked up with a man. The people at school were like a family. If someone became ill or had a baby, they would receive some type of gold gift.

"Why do you wear silver, Ms. Theresa?" my favorite staff member asked.

"I just like silver." I responded.

"You know women wear gold because gold make you look sexy" she said mysteriously as if she was telling me a secret. All the Muslim women at work wore only gold bracelets, necklaces, watches or rings. I guess they wanted to look sexy.

The girls in the upper grades were required to cover their hair. One of my colleagues stated that the girls begin to wear an Abaya once they begin their menstrual cycle. That begins their passage into womanhood which is similar to American culture. All the different school levels wore a school uniform. In the United States having students wear uniforms was always a hassle on any school level. Here it is mandated. There was a distinct similarities and differences between the Emirati women and the women of the United States. They both loved and indulged in cosmetics, fashion, and perfume. The outer beauty was just as important as the inner beauty.

Schooling in the UAE

This year my school went through an inspection, which happens every two years for schools that are a part of Abu Dhabi Education and Knowledge. The inspection reminded me of the school accreditation process in the United States. I went through the accreditation process numerous times showing a large amount of documentation that included student achievement data, school evaluation assessment, and the school improvement plan. After our documents were received an inspection team of three showed up at the school where they reviewed all the remaining documentation, interviewed parents, interviewed staff members, and visited classes. The team spent three to five days at the school. After the inspection a report was sent to the school system and then to the school. This report will rate your school with a grade, which basically informs the public how well the school is meeting standard. In all, the process put a lot of pressure on everybody in the school system there. The difference between the process there and the one in the States is that a school could lose funding and close if it lost accreditation from the results of the inspection. This meant the stakes were extremely high. However, in the UAE, your school would only receive a rating. It would not close and no one would be fired. In short, schools in the UAE are very different than schools in America, though they all strive toward the same goal—that is, to be the best.

There were binders from the previous years of evidence collected by members of the staff to demonstrate the work of the school. The binders included all teacher evaluations, student data, communication, professional development, and more. The school had evidence for days and years. I was amazed at the overwhelming documentation of the school. During the inspection, the inspectors were expected to look through the documentation to support the overall comprehensive evaluation. This style of record keeping was antiquated. This information could easily be stored in a database system.

The students on the high school and middle school level do not transition to other classrooms. They stay in the same classroom while the teachers rotate to them. In the states we would call them teachers on a cart because they do not have their own classroom. Can you imagine what a high school or a middle school would be like if the children stayed in the same classroom all day and different teachers rotated in and out of the class? That can be very difficult for students and for teachers. At any rate, in the UAE, the work hours for each cycle are different. This was the first time in my life as an educator that I was able to drop my daughter off and pick her up from school and still be on time for work. When I worked in the states, I didn't have the time to drop her off at school and still make it to my school on time. And even in places where before and aftercare is necessary, it's usually less expensive. The US really has much higher costs of living in many ways. She had to attend before and after school care. On some days, I didn't get out of school in enough time to pick her up. It is a blessing to have the time to drop off your children and pick them up from school without missing work. The only time I could pick my children up from school in the United States was when I didn't go to work that day.

This was my 20th year as an educator, and I was spending it as a Vice Principal in an all pre-kindergarten and kindergarten school that was getting ready to go through a school inspection. When I first met the principal, whom I came to affectionately call Queen, made sure that I was aware of the school's current status from the previous inspection. The school had received a rating of A3 which meant the school was "Good." If a school received A2 that meant that they were "Very Good." If a school received an A1 that meant that it was "Outstanding." The principal wanted me to help bring the school to an A2 status. Schools that received high ratings were viewed by other schools and parents as a quality school. It brought positive publicity to the school and high accolades to the principal for leading the school. There were different categories that the school receives a rating for and then they receive an overall rating.

It was very evident that my principal had high standards for her school and the staff. She ruled quite differently from what I heard from my other administrator friends at other schools. The Queen did not tolerate tardiness, laziness, or excessive absenteeism. Everyone in the school was a part of the school improvement plan in some way, including the security guard.

The school was notified on a Monday that the inspectors would be at the school on Sunday. The school week began on Sunday and ended on Thursday. The school had anticipated the inspection and was ready; however, that didn't stop the level of anxiousness among the staff. The students were none the wiser as they should be. The inspection team included three former educators. Two of them were English speaking and one was Arabic speaking. The Arabic speaking inspector observed the Arabic courses and the other two inspectors observed the English taught courses. Each day I met the lead inspector because my principal was out due to unforeseen circumstances. Hopefully Inshallah we will receive a good report. Inshallah is a term I never heard until I moved to the middle east. Inshallah means, "God willing" or "If God wills." I started saying it so much that I wondered if God thought I was abusing His will. While in the UAE, I heard things like, "I will call them tomorrow, Inshallah."

"The parents will come to the meeting, Inshallah."

"The school buses will be on time, Inshallah."

Students begin studying the Quran in KG 1 which is pre-kindergarten. They attend Masjid at the school on a weekly basis. Masjid is another word for Mosque. Masjid is a carpeted room in the school where the students and teacher take off their shoes before entering. Islamic Muslim lessons are held in Masjid. Students as young as four were able to recite scriptures and prayers in the Quran. The studies of the Quran continue as a student matriculates through the school system. It was quite impressive to see a five-year-old recite the Quran with so much emotion and articulation.

It was obvious with the social studies curriculum in pre-kindergarten, students are taught at a very early age to love everything UAE. I had never seen such patriotism for a country as I saw in the schools in the United Arab Emirates. The schools had huge celebrations for Flag Day and the day the country was established. As the anniversary of the founding day of the country every other car in the school's parking lot was decorated with the UAE flag or a picture of the first president of UAE posted on the side or back. All the Muslim teachers had their cell phone case decorated with the UAE flag or pictures of one of the Sheiks.

The school calendar showed students' last day would be July 5th though the school knew the students would stop coming to school during Ramadan so they instructed teachers to finish teaching the curriculum prior to the holiday. After Ramadan, the students would still have a month of school left, but they wouldn't come, beginning their summer early. For this reason, teachers rushed and crammed as much information as they could into only a few weeks. It was like teaching an eight-week course in two to three weeks. As a result, there was some cheating that was taking place, which was so widespread that the newspaper wrote an article about it.

Several administrators talked about all the students writing the exact same thing for the writing portion of the tests. The practice writing prompts were the exact same writing prompts that were on the test . It was stated that parents worked as a group to help students memorize and write the exact same things. It was very apparent that the students had put no thought into their writing whatsoever.

Most of the school programs include the students wearing clothing and performing dances that represent the country. Imagine the United States celebrating the Fourth of July every week is what the patriotism is like in the UAE. The affinity that the people have for the first president and the country is like nothing I've ever seen. No one ever talks bad about the Sheiks or the country.

I can see why they love the country so much. It would be hard not to love someone or something that takes care of you and provide for you. The government pays for them to have a house. The Emiratis just started paying for water and electricity the past two years. Before that, the government had provided water and electricity to all Emiratis. Once an Emirati man and woman marry, they can have the government build them a house or they can have the government give them land, where they would then build their own house.

Once a woman gives birth, the government pays the Emirati husband 600 AED ($160 USD) a month until the child marries or begins work. So, imagine if a woman has four small children, the husband would receive an extra 2400 AED ($650 USD) to his salary. Government taxes, medical insurance, and other fees are not taken out of his check. Their children don't pay for school or college. However, if they decide to earn a masters or additional degrees, they would have to pay. If a woman and husband divorce, the government will pay the woman that is not working 600 AED until she remarries. If they have a baby at the local hospital, Emiratis don't pay anything. People that rely on the government for housing and medical care are looked down upon in the United States, but it is expected that the government will take care of them in the United Arab Emirates. I see clearly why the people love the country so much!

The school system also influences the community by teaching students to respect others. One day a friend of mine who is also an administrator from the United States was in a salon where a Pilipino worker said that she was happy that the school system brought teachers from the west to teach. My friend was puzzled because she knew the lady could not afford to have her kids live in the UAE and pay for private school. So, she asked, "Why?" The lady said, "Because Westerns teach the children to treat everybody with respect and they treat us with more respect since there are more western teachers." We were both dumbfound at the statement. Meanwhile, in the United States two black men were arrested just for sitting in a Starbucks waiting for a friend. Two black men were asked to leave a L.A. Fitness just for working out. A Whitehouse aide is caught making insensitive and offensive comments about an American war hero and refused to publicly apologize. Meanwhile, western teachers are being praised for teaching Arabic children how to treat everyone with respect. The point is no matter where they are in the world, people want to be treated with respect. I have not experienced any racist comments or remarks while living in the UAE. I did hear, however, that some people are treated with less respect based on their nationality.

Expats had to send their children to private schools, as they are not allowed to attend government schools. Some companies give their employees a tuition stipend for their children's school. I received a 20 percent discount on Chelsea's tuition. Tuition can be very expensive depending on where you live, not necessarily the quality of education a child receives. Tuition in Abu Dhabi City could cost about twenty thousand or more. I paid about 8 thousand for Chelsea's tuition for the year. After paying for her tuition, we still had enough money to live and travel.

As I was growing up, my mother taught me to treat everyone with respect no matter their position, race, or title. Everyone deserves to be respected. My mother did not allow my siblings and me to disrespect adults. I try my best to teach my children the same. I have taught them to treat people the way you would want to be treated. This is the mantra people should embody. People that are hurting tend to hurt other people. Although there was a language barrier at work.

Working in the UAE, I felt very respected by the teachers and students. I felt that most teachers in the UAE and the U.S. had a lot of respect for me because I was fair, knowledgeable, and people found it easy to talk to me. As I was in the desert supporting the children in the Middle East, I was constantly missing my son in the states. Rylan was a constant thought as I observed children so close to his age. I couldn't wait to see him again.

A Local Wedding

My neighbor turned girlfriend invited me and two other ladies to a wedding of a staff member's sister I was super excited, and I couldn't wait to attend. I'd heard the Emiratis spared no expense when it came to weddings. I'd heard the weddings were very elaborate and the women were a lot looser and partied a lot at the weddings. I couldn't wait to see these women dance and let loose. The wedding décor was breathing-taking and overwhelming, yet very elaborate. The ceiling was draped in large pieces of silk and chiffon fabric attached to huge oversized crystal chandeliers. The tables were all wooden white, trimmed in gold metal. They all looked like Egyptian art and too pretty to eat on. The tables were all U-shaped that spilled out from the catwalk stage. The table settings included huge colorful flowers, candelabras draped in pearls and live beautiful pastel-colored flowers.

The lighting décor reminded me of something from a movie scene. There were lights affixed to certain areas and other lights danced across the silk hanging fabric.. Bright blue, soft red, and soft white lights danced against the tables and walls. The center pieces were all made with beautiful live roses and calla lily flowers spilled over the vase as if to allow wedding guests to get a whiff of their relaxing and soothing smell. The men and women entered the wedding hall through separate doors.

As I entered the wedding hall, I was greeted by a line of women dressed in their fancy, black Abayas and Shaylas. Some of the older women wore the metal face garment that covered their nose and across their cheekbones. I never understood the purpose of wearing the face mask. Next, I was greeted by a line of older women who appeared to be 60 or above. I only say that because you could see the deep wrinkles in their faces. There were a few younger women in the welcome line of women, but not many. The custom called for shaking the hand of each lady and giving a cheek-to-cheek kiss. There is a long catwalk stage and in the center of the stage was a luxurious emperor style couch on the stage. The couch was laced with beautiful soft pink and white flowers. There was a huge backdrop of flowers behind the couch. The flower-laden couch is almost the first thing you see when you enter the main area. This is where the bride and groom will briefly sit. Children in attendance were dressed like little showcase dolls, with their nannies right behind them making sure they are not too busy.

The table was full of Arabic food which was served by one of the serving staff assigned to each table. I'm not really a fan of Arabic food, but I did partake in the dinner. Arabic food tasted bland. My palate wasn't stimulated by its boring flavors. Also, there were tables with large amounts of chocolate candies. In addition, uniform staff walked around with a large tray of chocolate for people to enjoy. There were several ladies dressed in uniform that stopped at each table several times to offer different smelling perfumes and oils to put on. They wore a facial expression that said, "Please try this perfume so I can be the first person to finish my oils and perfumes."

There were two large screens on each side of the stage that showed a video of the groom and men dancing on the other side. The men appeared to be having a really good time. Most of the men were dressed in white Kanduras and head wraps. Only a few wore tan Kanduras. They danced in a line with canes, which is the traditional style dance celebration. Seeing them dance reminded me of the fraternity men of Kappa Alpha Psi when they stroll. The men twirled canes between their fingers and rolled the cane over their shoulders as they danced in a line side by side. The men are smiling and laughing and talking to one another.

As for the women, they did their dancing on the stage to Arabic music. They were having fun, but it didn't compare to the men's good times. Some of the women had taken off their dreary, black Abayas and Shayla to show off their sparkling long dresses. All the dresses were different in style and color. Some sported lace and a low-cut cleavage, which surprised me. Some were fitted to show off their hourglass shapes. I assumed that hat most of the women who did not have on an Abaya were close family members of the bride and groom. I was in amazement when I saw the hourglass shapes topped off by extremely long hair that extended to their waistline. Their well-made up faces had me thinking they were headed to a Hollywood movie red carpet premier. They reminded me of Kim Kardashian, but were much prettier, with bodies never saw a plastic surgeon. I was really baffled that they got all dressed up and didn't interact with any men. In fact, the only men who have seen them without an Abaya and their natural hair is their husband, brother, or father. The entire wedding was segregated by sex.

Shortly after we all began mingling and eating, an announcement was made in Arabic and the lights were dimmed and special smoke effect filled the room. After the announcement, all the women that were not wearing an Abaya quickly grabbed their Abaya and Shayla to cover. The bride entered the hall alone and walked up the stairs of the catwalk to each side of the room. Everyone is taking pictures of her including the professional photographer. I couldn't help but wonder who would look at the photo album. The women are always covered so I can only assume her mother, female family members, and female friends will view the final wedding album. The bride wore an amazing white beaded wedding gown with an extra-long train. The train had to be at least 10 feet long. She wore a nervous smile I could understand her nervousness. After all, this would be her first time meeting her husband and spending time with him alone. I don't think I could ever be involved in an arranged marriage. However, I have heard of some men and women would converse prior to getting married. They could also meet one another face-to-face, but only in the presence of their parents.

This culture does not allow dating of any kind. I was told by several Emirati Muslim women that the groom's mother will contact the bride's mother to say that her son would like to marry her daughter. Then the bride's family will conduct their research on the groom and inform the bride of their findings. Their research may have involved finding out if he'd been married before, has children? Will she be a second wife? Does he attend the mosque frequently? What does he do for a living? The bride will then decide if she would like to marry him. Also, she depends heavily on her brother and father's information about the man she will marry. Getting married is a major thing in the Emirati Muslim culture. Most of the men and women of the Emirates marry their cousins. In this culture, it is acceptable to marry your cousin. I heard about things like that, but I thought it was all talk and not a common thing. However, it is quite common in the Emirati culture to marry your first cousin or second cousin.

After the long picture-taking session, an announcement was made, and just like that, the women put on their abayas and Shayla because the groom is coming. The groom entered with two other gentlemen (sometimes, the groom may enter with his mother.) They all go on to the stage to greet the bride and more pictures are taken. After the picture taking, the groom left. I was told that he will take the bride with him. However, most of the wedding guests left prior to the groom entering. It seemed like the wedding is more of a quiet get together than a big celebration. I was told that another party takes place the next day or so where the bride and women in her family will wear all their gold.

Going to this wedding was a special insight into the local culture that I was delighted to be invited. I had two other occasions when I was invited to weddings, and each was amazing. However, this wedding involved six brides getting married at the same time in the same location. One of them was a sister of a co-worker. I had invited two of my girlfriends to attend. When we entered, we shook hands with a line of older women. This wedding was not as elaborate and intimate as the other weddings. This one took place in a large conference center hall. Before this wedding, I had never seen so many women that had snatched waistlines. It was very evident that a lot of the women had plastic surgery to contour their waistlines, big butt, and big hips. Many wore contact lenses to change their eye color. You could tell the women that were related to the brides. They all had on makeup that made them look like drag queens. I didn't even recognize my coworker until she came closer to me. Their make-up was two to three shades lighter than their skin and was very thick. I had just seen one of the brides a couple of days ago, but when she walked down the catwalk, I didn't recognize her. All six of the brides looked exactly same in the face. They all had on the exact same style make-up. My girlfriends and I were in complete shock.

I asked a colleague that was sitting next to me if she thought the women looked alike. I wanted to make sure that I was seeing this correctly. She said it was because they all had the same makeup.

"Do you think some of the women had surgery?"

"Lots of surgery!"

"Why would they have surgery and then cover it up with an abaya?"

"Because if a man, mother or sister sees them, then they would want her for their son or brother."

I was speechless. The women were getting all this plastic surgery to show it off to other women, so the women would then choose them to be a wife for their son. That was the first time I had ever heard that mentioned. I would never have thought that these pious women would use plastic surgery to change the look of their body and face. I guess they were no different than any of the American women I knew that used plastic surgery. Many of the women in the United States had engaged in weight loss surgery while they were overseas.

The Emirati weddings are very different than the traditional U.S. wedding. I'm told by other Muslim women from other countries like Egypt and Jordan that they celebrate with men and women at weddings. However, one thing that does remain constant in the Muslim culture is that prior to the wedding celebration, the bride and groom sign a marriage contract. The marriage contract includes things the bride and groom would like. Some things could include all new wardrobe for the bride, all new furniture for the bride, and an opportunity for the bride to finish college. My teacher's sister requested that they move into their own home. She didn't want to live in the same home with her husband and his family. I found that to be very interesting. I was thinking what man wouldn't want his wife to be educated. I wondered if there were some things in my own marriage contract that I wanted, would I still be married. The Muslims rarely get divorced, though divorce does exist.

Because I was living in UAE with my daughter, they assumed I was married. Divorce is not even a thought until you tell them you are divorced. A lot of times when I conducted business and they saw Chelsea, they asked, "Where is husband?" Sometimes I would respond, "Working in America" or "I'm divorced." I had to take Chelsea to the doctor and I told the receptionist that I was divorced, and she looked at me like I was crazy and kept referencing my husband. I guess once you get married, that man or woman is always your spouse in the eyes of God and the Muslim people. I had no real feelings about it. However, I would say that being divorce made me feel like I was worthy of being married in UAE. The culture put such a big emphasis on marriage that if a woman wasn't married by a certain age she was frowned upon or was viewed differently.

The women in the UAE are groomed to marry very young. Some of my staff members got married as young as 15. The women opt to get married young because they run the risk of not marrying an Emirati. When women marry outside of their nationality, their children will take on the nationality of the father. So, for example, if an Emirati woman marries and have children with a man from Yemen, her children will have a Yemen passport even though she has a United Arab Emirate passport. However, if an Emirati man marries and has children from a Yemen woman, then the children would receive a United Arab Emirates passport. One of the benefits in both situations is that the children would be allowed to attend government schools. Having an Emirates passport would afford the children more government benefits than those children without one. The importance of marriage was obvious in a land that was so foreign to me. In the UAE, if a woman was married, she was viewed as one that was worthy and set on a pedestal. She was given a level of respect that was understood. This was very different than the culture that I was accustomed to in the United States. Women that were independent and self-sufficient were viewed as strong, confident, and respected. Married life attributed to different cultures in two different countries.

When Chelsea and I first arrived in the UAE we would see these massive homes that looked like mini mansions. We thought that was a lot of house for one family. To my surprise there are usually more than one family that lives in those homes. One large house could include four different families. All the ladies that were married all lived with their husbands' family. None of the women lived in their own home with just their husband and children. So, the houses were huge. They all had very similar styles. The front of the house included very large pillars and a grand front entrance. The homes had their own wing, but they shared the common areas such as living room, kitchen, dining room, and Majilis rooms. Majilis is an Arabic term for "a place of sitting." So, there would be two Majilis rooms, one for men and one for women. Remember the men and women do not socialize together. A staff member shared that during Ramadan, the men ate in a separate area from the women.

Traditionally, the married women would visit their parents' home weekly. Family traditions and family values are very important in the UAE Muslim culture. I've asked several of the women how is this done when the man has multiple wives. Depending on the situation, the wives leave together and some live separate. The husband will then split his time between the two or three or four wives. Sometimes the children knew all of their siblings and sometimes they didn't. A friend shared a story of a man picking up one of his kids from school and he literally couldn't remember which kid. It is not uncommon for the men to have 10 or more children. Remember the government pays the man for each child that he has, and he is still married to the child's mother.

Their cultures and traditions are very dear to them. As an outsider looking in it was very hard for me to relate. I liked my privacy and space. So, living in the house with multiple families would not work for me. I asked one of the ladies at my job if she wanted her space sometimes. She said that she will just stays in her room and there are days that go by when she doesn't see her sister-in-law.

The women of UAE enjoyed and cherished smelling like the finest fragrances. The ladies at work engaged in the use of Bakhoor. It is the process of burning woodchips that have been soaked in different oils or fragrances. Oud is one of the most famous scents in UAE. When they burn the woodchips, the women will put the canister that burns the chips under their Abayas, over their Shaylas, under their arms, and under their hair. One day I walked into my principal's office and saw one of the staff members kneeling with the bakhoor canister holding it under the principal's Abaya. The fumes were going under her Abaya leaving an oud and rubbing alcohol smell. Initially I was surprised, but then it became a part of the morning tradition of the school. I guess the principal could see the surprise and puzzled look on my face. She said in her Arabic accent, "This is part of my culture Ms. Theresa." "Do you have culture in America?" "What do tradition and culture do you have in America?" I really didn't know what to say because I was so stunned by what I just saw. However, I was able to questionably say, "We have traditions and culture." I knew when it came out my mouth is sounded crazy. I wanted to say, "The Europeans stole all our cultures and traditions when they killed and sold my ancestors into slavery."

I gave the staff member the nickname "Bakhoor Girl." It was like once she came around with the bakhoor everyone had a different kind of vibe. Everyone seem to be more mellow and chill. They would burn the bakhoor in meeting rooms before a meeting. It really was like aroma therapy. The different woodchips and coals varied in cost just like perfume. The ladies would say, "Try it Ms. Theresa." "You will love it." They were right too. I got accustomed to the different smells. I would tell them which ones I liked and the ones I didn't like. If it was one that I didn't like, they would be sure to tell me that it didn't belong to them. It was funny how they didn't want to be the one known for the bakhoor smell I didn't like. One staff member even said in her Arabic accent, "Oh that's Naama's, not mine." "She bring that one."

The women would then spray on perfume on their clothes after getting the bakhoor. They all carried the regular sized perfume in their purse. One lady had two to three different bottles of perfume in her purse. They always wanted to get my opinion. It was like if the American girl like it, then it's a hit. They didn't care if you were already wearing your own perfume. They would say, "Try this Ms. Theresa." So of course, I would try it and give my opinion. If it was one I didn't like they would say in their Arabic accent, "Why you not like?" "This expensive." It was like they thought because it was expensive it must smell good. The women were just like the American women. They cared about themselves just as much as the women in America. They probably invested in beauty products, eyelash extensions, micro blading and cosmetic surgery more than American women.

CHAPTER 6

FIRST TRIP TO JORDAN

Two of my goals with taking the job in the UAE were to travel and pay off my credit cards. I couldn't wait to take my first trip. After waiting a month, I finally received my passport back with my residential visa attached to one of the pages. I was finally able to leave the country and take a mini trip somewhere. Because Chelsea still had not received her residential visa, we had to do what is called border run. A border run is when you exit or leave the country to enter another country and turn around and re-enter the country. Chelsea had to do two border runs to Oman as we went through the process of getting her residential visa. Chelsea was adapting a lot better than I had expected. I thought she would get homesick and miss her brother and father. However, Chelsea was a lot more resilient than I imagined. She was a very outgoing child that would talk to just about anybody. Most of the expatriates that were staying in the hotel met Chelsea before they met me. I guess you're wondering how was that possible. Chelsea was an adventurous kid that loved swimming. While staying at the Danat Hotel in Al Ain she frequented the pool and socialized with all the hotel guests. People would speak to Chelsea and then turn to me and say, "You must be Chelsea's mom, we met her in the pool." She really enjoyed the Danat Hotel, but we would laugh and call it the DoNot Hotel. We called it that because although the pictures made it look extremely nice, it really needed some updates. The hotel rugs looked very worn, and the bathroom could've used some updated hardware. However, it was our home for at least two weeks. We used a laundry service to wash, dry, and fold our clothes. We learned about the service from the other expatriates. The water was so harsh that it took no time for our clothes to lose their vivid bright colors. I ended up purchasing a shower filter for our bathrooms once we moved. However, I don't think it made a difference on our skin or hair. A lot of people complained about how bad the water was on their hair. My Egyptian neighbor complained how the water made her hair shed constantly.

Still, she and I were able to take our first trip. Chelsea and I took our first trip to the country Jordan, another Muslim country in the middle east. We traveled to Jordan right after school on a Thursday. My work week was from

Sunday to Thursday. We paid a driver to take us from Al Ain to Dubai International Airport. We flew into Amman, Jordan on Fly Dubai airline. Fly Dubai is a budget airline in the middle east. Our trip to Jordan was a total of $700 USD. The flight lasted about 3 hours. We were so excited. Chelsea and I both did research on the country prior to traveling. We knew we wanted to see Petra, the Dead Sea, and Jesus' Baptism Site. However, we saw that and more. When we first arrived in the airport, I had to purchase a visa for Chelsea and me. The visa cost about $75 USD each. We had a driver named Haroon who was highly recommended and served as our driver the entire trip. Chelsea's eyes lit up when she received her second international stamp. She had the biggest smile on her face when the airport personnel stamped her passport. I took her picture. She was excited and ready to take on the country Jordan.

We arrived late at night and our driver drove us to Petra which was a 3-hour drive. Chelsea stuck to me like glue in the van. She didn't appear to be afraid, but I could tell by her closeness to me she had some reservations and wanted to stick right by my side. There were a lot of curves and bumpy roads. We got a little nervous at times because we had no idea where we were, and we had just met the driver for the first time. I will admit that meeting a driver in a foreign country for the first time can be a little scary. My only communication prior to our arrival was via Whatsapp. We didn't take the journey alone. Two of my neighbors and another expatriate joined in on the trip. In total there were four adult females and three children. I told my family where we were going, but they didn't have any details. I now realize that I should've given more details about our trip to my family and friends in the United States.

Chelsea nor I didn't know what to expect in Jordan. All we knew that it was another Muslim country that was frequently visited by expatriates living in Abu Dhabi. Our first hotel was booked at the last minute due to a mix up of me booking the wrong location of another hotel. We arrived at the hotel at about 1:00 AM in the morning. The hotel was old and very dated. It was nestled in the mountains of Petra. Incidentally, Petra is where they filmed *Indiana Jones the Last Crusade*. We were greeted by the hotel manager, Abraham and 8 champagne glasses filled with what we thought was champagne. To our disappointment, it was juice. The juice tasted pretty sweet and had a nice chill. However, it was perfect for the post adventurous drive to the hotel. Abraham was very welcoming and quite flirtatious with me. He smiled at me a little bit more than he smiled at the other ladies. He even asked if we could talk more via WhatsApp. I didn't want to say no so I exchanged information with him on WhatsApp, but I wasn't interested in getting to know him more. I had no desire in dating.

After returning from Jordan, I kept getting messages from the hotel manager, Abraham. He wanted me to return to Jordan by myself. He explained that he really wanted to show me the beauty of Jordan. The messages were coming via an app called IMO. He was even more flirtatious. I thought it was cute at first. I was not dating anyone or even entertaining the thought of dating anyone. So, I enjoyed the attention. Most of my comments were "Thank you for the compliment." You can never give a woman too many genuine compliments. However, it became a little annoying.

We had to walk up two flights of stairs to get to our hotel room. Our room had two twin beds. The sheets were dingy and there was one small window. When we looked out the window, it was pitch black. We thought it was just a wall starring back at us. However, we learned in the morning that the window was crouched in between two walls. Broken bricks and wires were exposed everywhere. We joked that it reminded us of a military scene of the aftermath of a bombing. We could hear and see the pigeons flying back and forth between the small walls. Chelsea was a great traveling partner. She didn't complain about much.

Once we got dressed, we went out on the terrace and could see the houses built into the mountains at a distance. The scenery was quite amazing with the son rising as well. I don't recall seeing as many Mosques as I did in Al Ain. The hotel manager named Abraham was very nice. He was quite flirty, but he really wanted us to go onto Trip Advisor and give a high rating. The hotel was a two-star, but it did provide a shelter for a short period of time. The hotel served breakfast that I didn't like. Middle Eastern food was just not pleasing to my palate. I learned later when I almost passed out that I should've eaten. We traveled to Jordan with five other people. There was a total of four adults and three children on this trip. Haroon was at the hotel bright and early as expected to take us to Petra. I was hoping we would pass a store on the way to grab a pastry, but we didn't.

Petra was very different than the United Arab Emirates. The local people in Jordan didn't really like their government. Haroon shared that the government took all the money from the citizens and didn't really help the citizens. The same sentiments are felt in the United States. On the other hand, the Emiratis loved their government and the Sheiks. Petra, which means "rock" in Greek, and is known as one of the seven wonders of the world. It is a city that was carved out of sandstone. Petra was built by a nomadic Arab tribe known as the Nabataeans centuries before Christ. When we arrived at the site, we met with a tour guide that was set up by Haroon. The tour guide explained the architecture and the history of the city. To get to the actual architecture, we had to ride a horse or walk. Because we were there for a short period of time, we opted to take the horse to save time.

I was nervous at first because the last time Chelsea attempted to ride or even be near a horse, it was a nightmare. It was at Girl Scouts Mom and Me Camp. It was time for us to go into the stable and she squeezed my arm and began crying shouting "no"! and that she didn't want to see the horses. Fast forward four years later, she is now facing a fear of riding a horse. She grabbed my hand and said, "Mommy, I'm riding with you." However, the horses were too small to accommodate two people, so she had to ride by herself. I was praying to God that she would ride by herself because I didn't want to walk a half mile in flat sandals in the heat. The temperature was nice. There was a nice cool breeze at 7:00 AM, but we I knew that would not remain. When she saw the horses were small, and someone would be there to guide the horses, her fears faded. My baby girl mounted a horse and rode it by herself for half a mile. The smile on her face was as bright as the sun shining on a sunny day. She held the straps of the horse so tightly as she yelled, "Look, Mommy!" I was able to take a couple of pictures to memorialize the experience. I was so proud to see her conquering her fear of riding horses.

After the short ride on the horses, we walked down a dirt road through narrow mountains to a large opening of the city of Petra. It was breathtaking to see the architecture of these buildings, such as the treasury, houses, tombs, and churches built out of sandstone. As we walked along the paths, several children stopped us to purchase their different trinkets. The tour guide recommended that we not purchase from them because they will not attend school and will remain peddling tourists instead of going to school. There were a few families that sold clothing and souvenirs. It was hard to believe that there were families that lived in the cave areas. We were told that the government provides a supplement for the families. They could move, but they were so attached to the land and didn't want to move. Later we had the option to ride donkeys up a mountain to view more architecture of the sandstone city.

We went from riding horses to riding donkeys in the city of Petra. The mountains had very jagged steps which made it difficult to ride the donkey up hill; however, we stayed the course and so did the donkeys. The guides recommended that we lean forward as the donkey trudged up the steep mountain. The path had narrow pathways; it was only the grace of God that we didn't fall over the cliff. I was so nervous. Again, Chelsea had to ride a donkey alone because of the size. I prayed that nothing happened to us and called on God and Jesus aloud as the donkeys made their way uphill and downhill. Once we got to the top of the mountain, there was more to explore. However, I began to feel extremely lightheaded and faint. I had to sit down because I was seconds from passing out. Luckily there was a concession stand that sold water, chips, juice, peanuts, and other snacks. Also, there was a shaded sitting area for people to rest. I took advantage of the concessions and sitting area. There was so much more to explore at Petra that we didn't see due to the time constraints. We will revisit again someday.

The Dead Sea

As we began driving to our next hotel, which was two to three hours away, Haroon showed us the Dead Sea. The Dead Sea is a hypersaline body of water, which means there are no living forms there due to the high levels of salt. The Dead Sea was beautiful. It reflected the clouds and sun as if it were a large mirror. The orange, blue, and gray colors shimmered on the dead sea were a reminder of God's work. We couldn't resist the opportunity to take pictures with the Dead Sea reflecting God's nature in the background. Haroon even pointed out a stone statue. The statue is known as Lot's wife as she was turned to a pillar of salt when she disobeyed God's order not to look back. The stoned statue looked just like someone turning around.

The next morning, we took a short walk from the hotel to take a dip into the Dead Sea. The second night we stayed at Movenpick. The Dead Sea was in the backyard of Movenpick. People were using the mud made from the dirt and water to cover their body. There was a life guard to help people in and out of the Dead Sea. The rocks are coated with thick layers of salt which made getting in and out of the Dead

Sea very slippery. If you have any cuts and I mean any cuts, don't get into the water. Chelsea had a cut on her leg and she quickly exited the water when she felt the burn. You cannot sink in the Dead Sea. We took all kinds of pictures lying on our back with our feet and hands up as if we were lying in a beach chair. This was one of the coolest experiences. Afterwards, we took some of the mud with us because it is supposed to be good for your skin.

Conquering Fear and the Roman Theater

Moving to a foreign place can be quite scary especially when you don't know what to expect. Seeing Chelsea riding the horse and conquering her fear reminded me of how fear can paralyze us, but we must push through. Fear can stop you from living the life God intended for you. Fear can stop you from living your best life. Chelsea taught me that, when faced with fear, I must talk myself through it. I'm reminded of the time Chelsea was afraid to come into our apartment in the states because there was a cat nearby. It was late at night and when I pulled into the parking space, she immediately noticed the cat sitting on the grass. The cat's eyes were twinkling in the night's sky. He reminded me of the neighbor who sat on the porch watching cars drive by. I had seen the cat numerous times and would walk by and ignore him. As I commenced to get out the, Chelsea yelled, "No, mommy! There is a cat out there!" I assured her that the cat didn't want anything from us and I got my things and started to go up the stairs. I thought she was behind me, until she screamed for me to help her out of the car. I refused and told her multiple times to just run up the stairs to our two-bedroom apartment. She would yell back, "No!" After a couple of times trying to convince her, I turned and started to walk up the stairs. About 30 minutes later, Chelsea came running into the apartment breathing heavily.

"Mommy, I did it! I talked myself through it. I kept saying, 'come on, Chelsea. You can do it! You can do it! Just run up the stairs and don't look at the cat."

I was so proud of her. Not only did she learn how to encourage herself when facing her fears, but also, she applied the skill of self-talk. This journey taught us both how to conquer our fears.

It is important that you learn how to motivate yourself even when you don't feel like it. To this day, when I'm running and want to stop, I think about Chelsea encouraging herself and I begin to encourage myself to keep running until I have accomplished my three-mile goal. So many people missed out on mega opportunities because they were afraid of what people would say, do, or think. I don't have a lot of fears. My mother would always tell people that I didn't fear anything. She would boast that as a toddler, I would walk around the house in the dark. I can't imagine what was going on in my head, but I've never been afraid of the dark.

Jordan was our first experience out of the United Arab Emirates. The people were friendly. We ate at a couple of restaurants that served Egyptian food. Because I wasn't a fan of middle eastern food, I only liked the salads. The Egyptians always referred to us as, "sister." The Filipinos always referred to us as "mom." In the southern part of the United States, I would be referred to as "ma'am." Every region had their own way of addressing you.

During our time in Jordan, we learned that the Romans once ruled the land. Haroon took us to a Roman Theater. It was incredible. The theater was built during the reign of Marcus Aurelius (169-177 AD). The theater is extremely large and steep. It seated about 6000 people. It was built and purposely built facing north to keep the sun off the spectators. The concrete stairs are extremely jagged and there are no handrails. The steepness of the theater can be quite scary once you climb to the top. The highest section of the seating was known as the "The Gods." This was extremely high; however, you could see and hear people on the stage perfectly. A freelance tour guide pointed out that if you stood in the center of the stage and spoke, it sounded like you were speaking into a microphone. The theater's precision to architecture and mathematical practice allowed for this little trick. It was quite incredible to think about how math precision played a major role in the design of the Roman theaters. Actors could be heard from all over the theater due to mathematical acoustics and architecture. There was special seating built into the theater for the king and queen which was much lower.

Chelsea and I enjoyed taking pictures in the king and queen seats. We even climbed all the way to the top of the theater on the jagged stairs. Looking out and down scared us due to the steepness. However, the view was well worth the adventure. The view from the top was spectacular. We met a couple of young boys that were from Iraq who asked to take pictures with us. They stated that they had never met black people before. That was quite interesting. I don't think living in the United States I was ever in awe about seeing another nationality or race. As

Chelsea and I traveled more; we experienced a lot of people wanting to take pictures with us. The challenge or fear for us was walking down the stairs of the theater and not falling, killing ourselves or causing a major injury. We were both nervous. My heart was beating fast and I knew I couldn't treat these like normal stairs and just walked down. So, I did as toddler would do. I sat down on my buttocks and scooted down the stairs. We laughed at ourselves looking like big babies, but it was the best way to get down those stairs and conquering our fear. As I mentioned before, fear can paralyze you, but you have to push through.

Sometimes I ask myself if I could've endured this journey alone. Having Chelsea to experience this with me was so rewarding. To hear her thoughts and outlook on life was exciting. She's so optimistic about her future. She goes from wanting to be the best Olympic swimmer and beat Michael Phelps's record for gold medals to wanting to design her own fashion merchandise. In the midst of it all, I've learned not to impose my views or prophesy over her life. I just pray that she enjoys life and live it the way God intended. I've seen children go down paths that many parents wished they had not gone down. These are children from two-parent households that society would deem to be successful citizens. However, children can be like animals, unpredictable.

Jesus' Baptismal Site

The country of Jordan is known for many historical landmarks. The north part of the country can boast about being the homeland of Prophet Elijah, and the northern and central regions take pride in Christ performing many miracles there. The country of Jordan offers so many historical sites you read about in the bible. Chelsea and I had the opportunity to visit the baptism site of Jesus. The baptism site is located very close to the Jordan River. A short distance on the other side of the river was Jerusalem. I never thought in my wildest dreams that we would see the Jordan River. I only read about Jerusalem and the Jordan River in textbooks and the bible. There were people being baptized in the Jordan River in Jerusalem. I posted a picture of us at the baptism site of Jesus on Facebook and the GPS tagged Jerusalem as our location. Many people thought we were in Jerusalem, but we weren't. I received a couple of instant messages that warned about the issue between Israel and the United Arab Emirates. It was forbidden for employees of Abu Dhabi Education Council to visit Israel and it could result in termination. I was not trying to get fired especially over a GPS malfunction.

The tour guide explained that they knew it was the site based on the description in the bible. I had to wrap my head around the fact that the country of Jordan was once predominately Christian but is now predominately Muslim. At the site, there is a mosaic art picture of one of the Catholic Pope's visit to the site.

According to the baptism website, the baptism site was a major Pilgrim Station from the days of John the Baptist. Even after he died, many of his students stayed in the area which was the birthplace of Christianity. Churches were built near the site, monks lived in caves, and pilgrims visited the site. This tradition continued until around the 14th Century. With the power of the Crusaders vanquished, and Byzantine weakening, the site was neglected, and the area returned under the control of local tribes. East of the Jordan was no longer a safe place to go, and with no guarantee of safety, pilgrimage to the site became less and less frequent, and then virtually stopped.

A scholar from Jerusalem discovered the Madaba Map [in Madaba present day Jordan], in 1897. This map was a 6th century Mosaic depicting a map of the Middle East in the 6th Century. The discovery and subsequent analysis of the map led to a renewed interest about the exact location of the Baptism Site. Pilgrims started to return to the area east of the River Jordan hoping to find clues to the location of the site.

Being at the site of Jesus' baptism was really intriguing and brought a sense of calm and togetherness between Chelsea and me. Chelsea wanted to be closer to me and hold my hand as we explored one of the nearby churches. She even shared an interest in wanting to be baptized, but not in the Jordan River. The water was very murky and was not pleasing to the eye. However, it presented a peace and calm. All the people on the tour took pictures and expressed experiencing a sense of calm. There was very little chatter. It was like we were all mesmerized by the site. After leaving the baptism site, we made our way to Mt. Nebo. If you thought the baptism gave a sense of calm, Mt. Nebo did that and more. Jordan had so many historical, biblical, and historical information we couldn't take it all in in one weekend. We noted that the people in Jordan spoke Arabic and English. Their English was decent unlike other countries we later visited. The language barrier posed serious issues for us in other countries.

Jordan was an exceptional trip for such a short period of time. There were so many things that we didn't get a chance to do. I would put it on the list of places to visit again. It really lit an international travel bug within Chelsea and me. To this day, Jordan was one of my favorite trips while living in the middle east.

Attention Deficit Hypertension Disorder Medication

Chelsea was diagnosed with Attention Deficit Hypertension Disorder when she was in her second semester of first grade. She's a bright girl and could easily interact with people from all backgrounds. She and my mother were so much alike. They never met a stranger. Her academics were always decent; however, her ability to stay focused was a serious struggle. Most people would say that is the case for many young children. In Chelsea's case, staying focused on a short story was hard. So, I decided to have her tested. I took her to see a child psychologist that diagnosed her with ADHD. I gave the medical records to her pediatrician, Dr. Ricketts. I really liked Dr. Ricketts because she only wanted the best for Chelsea and she stated that. "The medicine should only take the edge off and Chelsea had to use some of her own willpower to manager her behaviors." She also recommended that we use the name brand form of Adderall, not the generic. The name brand was much more expensive, and the insurance only covered a small portion. However, it was worth it if it would help her focus and not have any academic gaps. That is exactly what the medicine did, too! When Chelsea would take Adderall, she would be focused and get her work done with accuracy and precision. She really paid attention to detail. She would not be in a zombie state as I had seen some of my previous students who were on medication for ADHD. Her personality and self-esteem were intact.

When I decided to move to UAE, I asked the doctor to give me her medical records so that we could continue with her treatment plan there. We already had about a 30-day supply and the doctor wrote another prescription for 30 days. When we got to the UAE during the summer, Chelsea did not take her medicine. She only used the medicine during the school year and during the weekdays. She didn't take the medicine on the weekend. That was our way of giving her body a break from the medication. Once school started in UAE, she began taking the last bottle of Adderall. When I tried to get the U.S. prescription filled, the UAE hospital stated they would not fill it. The country saw the medication as a hard narcotic and wasn't suitable for children. So, I contacted Chelsea's pediatrician in the states and gave proof that I still had the prescription, and that the local pharmacist would not fill it, they wrote another prescription that her dad picked up and dropped off at the pharmacy. My dearest friend paid for the medicine and mailed it to me. When sending a package to the UAE, it must go through customs. If the package contains pills of any sort, it must be reviewed by the customs doctor. The customs doctor told me that the medication was not allowed in UAE and that I had to get a prescription signed and stamped by the local doctor stating that my daughter needed the medicine for them to give me the medication.

The local pediatrician referred us to the local child psychiatrist that was in the same hospital. The visit to see the psychiatrist was not covered for expatriates only for locals and I had to pay out of my pocket for the visit. The visit cost 850 AED which equaled about $230 USD. Yes, I paid that for a doctor visit. Once I received the prescription for the medication that was not allowed in the UAE and was being held by the customs doctor, I made my way back to the post office. I could not have a package delivered to me because we don't have physical addresses in the United Arab Emirates, only post-office boxes and customs would still open your package before they placed it in your P.O. Box. The customs doctor had to take a picture of the prescription send it to her manager who, in turn, sent it to the Ministry of Health who, in turn, granted us permission to receive the medication. We were warned that this would not be allowed again. That was fine with us because the psychiatrist was switching us to Conserta medication the next month.

The next month we took the prescription for Conserta to the hospital where the prescribing doctor saw patients. and we were told that they haven't had the medicine months and to try another local hospital. We took the prescription to be filled at another local government hospital. They stated that the medicine was a controlled substance and they had the medication. Chelsea and I were so relieved when the attendant stated that they had the medicine. Chelsea had been asking for the medicine because she was really having a hard time focusing and her grade in math was showing. Math was usually her strongest subject, but lately her attention to mathematical reasoning and accuracy was not there. The attendant left to speak with someone and came back and deflated our level of excitement. We were told that they could not fill the prescription because the prescription was not from one of their doctors. We would have to pay again to be seen by one of their doctors. The doctors were overbooked, and they would try to squeeze us in. We were told to come back on another day to see if another doctor would see us and we needed to bring all the information from the local doctor and the doctor from the states.

This was a major hassle. The entire process of trying to get Conserta took about a month. In the meantime, Chelsea was still attending school and her grades weren't the best and they weren't the worst. I was so exhausted running from pharmacy to pharmacy and doctor to doctor in 90 plus degree weather in a hot black Abaya. I had to do all of this after school hours when I wore an Abaya to work. Not because I had to, but it was easy and everyone at my school wore one. I remember breaking down in the car looking at Chelsea in the eyes as sweat beads dripped down my face. "Chelsea", I said, "you can do this! You are going to have to pray and meditate and ask God to help you focus. I'm sorry, but I just can't do it anymore!" I felt so bad, but I could not go to another place and get the runaround. I told her that we would begin to meditate together and limit her sugar intake and cut out all the foods with different dyes in them.

At that moment, she never asked for her medicine again and her grades were decent. I never received any calls from her teachers about her behavior or her missing work. I'm constantly encouraging her that she can do anything that she puts her mind to do. It was like all the praying and foods without all the extra additives helped her stay focused. She found a way to cope without the medication. I felt that the change in our diet helped as well. We didn't eat out at restaurants as much. We cooked a lot of our meals. Chelsea was learning to cook more and more. She found a love in the kitchen. She would bake a cake at least once or twice a month. She loved baking chicken in an oven bag with a special kind of seasoning. It was like she was growing up before my very eyes.

I listened to several audio books with her in the car. The greatest book that may have influenced her is the audio book, *The Secret*. During the time of listening to the book, she would hear segments about the power she has within herself to create the life that she desires. Every morning, we prayed that our day is blessed. I loved to hear her lead us in prayer. She always began by thanking God and then she asked God to bless her with specific things. She even asked God to help me, her brother, and her dad with specific things. I was so surprised one day when she prayed for my current principal. She had only met her once, but she heard me speak about her struggling with her health. Chelsea has a spirit that I truly admire. She has prayed for people at school like her teachers and even students that may have hurt her feelings. God is definitely in her heart.

Living in a Muslim country where the expectation is that Muslims pray five times a day has strengthened and matured Chelsea's and my communication with God. Hearing the constant prayer calls over the loud speakers from the mosque practically in my backyard is a constant reminder that we need to communicate with God on a regular basis. The dedication I saw for prayer in this country is remarkable. I saw men praying on their prayer rug on the side of the highway with cars speeding by them at 120 kilometers per hour. I even saw a man praying on his prayer rug right outside the ATM. I wondered if he was praying for more money.

People walked by him as if nothing was happening. I was in shock that no one did anything or even said "excuse me". I remember attending a soccer game in Al Ain and there was a large section of prayer rugs in the middle of the hall and men were praying on the rugs. They would say a prayer and then kneel to their knees and then their forehead and nose would touch the rug. There are eight positions that are done during the time of prayer. Also, each prayer has a name. The five prayers are Fajr, Dhuhr, Asr, Maghrib, and Isha'a. The time of day of the prayers change slightly depending on the location of the moon and sun. When Chelsea and I visited the Grand Mosque in Abu Dhabi City, there was a sixth prayer time posted. I asked one of the Muslim men working there about it. He stated it's a sixth prayer only for those that want to pray for extra blessing and points. There is a point system that I will speak about later. It's quite interesting and if you're a mathematical genius, you could keep up with it.

I never saw a woman go into a mosque. I asked a few ladies about why I never saw women go into a mosque and they said it was because women pray at home and that most mosques do not have a place for women to pray. The mosque tends to only have space for men to pray. I immediately thought that was unfair. I understood the notion of women and men praying in separate rooms, but the mosques should have a place for women to pray. Also, I was told that women that are menstruating are not allowed to go into the mosque.

They are seen as unclean. There are some prayer rooms for women and men in the malls and in select stores. I recall doing some furniture shopping and I went into a section and walked into a woman wearing a black abaya and shayla praying on her prayer rug right there between a bedroom set and living room furniture section. She had just finished and rose slowly to her feet. She gave the prayer rug to the sales associate. I thought the rug belonged to her, but it belonged to the store. I really felt like I was interrupting her time with God. I apologized to her and I made the comment that I should've been down there praying with her. She gave me the most pleasant smile. It was like she appreciated me for acknowledging and respecting her time with God.

I recall a time when I walked in on my principal praying in her office. I was with another staff member who wanted to obtain a binder off the principal's bookshelf. She walked in first as if she didn't see my principal fully covered in a black abaya and shayla sitting Indian style on her prayer rug. My eyes immediately got large and I said "oops" and began to turn back around and head out the office. The staff member said, "it's okay" and commenced to get the book off the shelf. My principal continued to silently pray as if she didn't hear or see us three feet away shuffling through books on her bookshelf. Then another staff member came in and stood about two feet from my principal waiting for her to finish her prayers to sign a document. I was in total shock. Growing up

Christian, I was taught that your time with God should be taken seriously. You are not allowed to enter the main chapel during prayer time. So, it's a similar ethos, but a different application. In other words, prayer is serious, but the building is seen as less important to the process. The Muslims did not share that same practice. They would pray anywhere, and it didn't matter who walked by or stood next to them. However, the person that is praying is the one that is taking the moment seriously because they are the one spending alone time with God, not the people outside of the prayer. It's almost like when I'm praying in my car talking to God and people are driving by blasting their music or having loud conversations, my respect and time for God at that moment is much bigger than people carrying on with their business around me. I'm sure at that moment God is only interested in my personal time with him and my personal time is truly between Him and me.

First Doctor Visit

There were times when Chelsea and I had to go to a dentist or doctor. Chelsea's first visit to the doctor's office was called a well visit. She started a new swim team in Dubai and had to get a physical and paperwork signed and stamped by a doctor. I made an appointment at Oasis Hospital in Al Ain for Chelsea to see the local pediatrician. There were three entrances to the hospital. There was an emergency entrance, an entrance for adults that took appointments, and a well entrance just for kids. Chelsea and I waited for about 20 to 30 minutes until we were finally called to the back. A nurse took her weight which was taken in kilograms. We had to use the conversion app I kept on my home screen to realize Chelsea hadn't gained a pound. She still weighed 39 kilograms which equaled about 85 pounds. She laughed and sighed at the same time because her younger brother still weighed more than her.

The waiting room was decorated in slightly faded orange colors that I think were once very bright. There was a kid-friendly mural and an English cartoon played on the tv monitor that hung from the wall. Children could play with the Lego like table toys or read one of the children's books in English and Arabic. The wide-eyed Indian pediatrician said, "Hello, how are you?" as if she just learned how to speak English. We understood her, and she asked us questions about where we were from and how long we lived in the UAE. She had been practicing in UAE for 12 years. She checked Chelsea's breathing and listened to her hear with a stethoscope. She was pleased and had nothing negative to say. She kept a smile on her face showing her spaced teeth. Chelsea and I both shared a glazed and dazed look on our face. I think it was because the pediatrician spoke to us as if we didn't understand English.

However, I think she just wanted to make sure she was speaking proper English. Most of her patients and their parents probably spoke Arabic.

CHAPTER 7

POLITICKING IN THE MIDDLE EAST

Even though we were away from home, that didn't stop us from hearing about all the different political battles that were taking place. The middle east had their own political battles to fight. I watched CNN and CNN International more now than ever before. It was one of the ways I still felt connected to home. To hear that Saudi Arabia's air defense forces intercepted a ballistic missile over Riyadh was quite alarming. Saudi Arabia was pretty close in distance to the UAE. A lot of the local Muslims in UAE had family that lived in the Kingdom of Saudi Arabia. According to an online news report, Yemen's Houthis had stepped up missile attacks on the kingdom in what was said to be retaliation for air raids by a Saudi-led coalition fighting the Iran-aligned armed movement. The attack brought me to the reality that there is no peace in the middle east.

President Trump of the United States didn't make it any better by moving the United States Embassy from Tele Viv to Jerusalem. Many of the Muslims that were from Palestine and Jordan was giving my coworkers and I the dirtiest looks. "It wasn't our fault; we weren't the ones that voted for Trump" I wanted to say. When it came to politics and freedom of press in the middle east, there was none. There was no such thing as the freedom of press. Everything that was published in the newspapers and online had to go through a government agency for approval.

Many of the expat administrators and teachers were upset about the changes that were occurring within the education system. They wanted to protest until they realized that was illegal and they would be put in jail. The country fired a college professor for teaching the journalist curriculum as it related to freedom of press. Needless to say, the professor wasn't employed much longer after that.

Many of the expats that were from the United States felt embarrassed about the political things that were taking place at home. The president and employees of the Whitehouse were making very inappropriate comments from mocking a war hero to calling all Latinos seeking an asylum thugs and gang members. The president was allowing children as young as 3 months to be separated from their parents at the border seeking an asylum. It was becoming very disheartening. I asked myself over and over if this was something I wanted to go back to. I even told God I wasn't ready to be thrown back into society that was so insensitive, and the spirit was nowhere present. As a matter of fact, the word of God was being manipulated to perpetuate such separations of children and their parents.

The education system in the United Arab Emirates involved a great deal of politics. There appeared to be a battle that was taking place at the top of the education organization. There appeared to be a power struggle between the Ministry of Education and Abu Dhabi Education Council. The schools were receiving extremely mixed messages as it related to the curriculum, resources, materials, and employment contracts, and more. All the correspondence that was emailed to the schools were all in Arabic. Prior to the merger the correspondence once in both Arabic and English.

There was an article that was released that expressed the frustration of the local Emiratis. They felt the education jobs were given to the western teachers leaving the locals unemployed. I wasn't aware of these views prior to working in the UAE. They were hiring so aggressively which didn't speak to a nationalist movement. The salary and credentials of a local teacher and western teacher were quite different. In the United States, teachers were required to have a teaching certification. That was not the case for the local teachers in the United Arab Emirates. The school system was at the beginning stages of implementing a teacher certification program. A leadership certification didn't exist.

The government encouraged teachers to obtain advance level degrees, yet they didn't have a teacher certification program. Two of my teachers were both receiving master's degrees in education. Both teachers were single. One was 28 years old and the other was 29 years old. When I asked them about getting married, they both weren't overly interested. One even said, "No I don't want to get married." The other one said, "I do want to be married." However, they understood getting married at their age was difficult. Most of the local Emirati women were married in their late teens early twenties. The traditions of the culture dictated a lot of the actions of the women. The country was slowly transitioning to Western ways and the restructuring of organizations which left many in limbo.

Living Life

Through our journey abroad, I shared some of our personal and professional experience on social media, and people would say things like, "Y'all are living." Heck, I even made comments like "We are living" or #livingourbestlife. I like to think we are all living in our own way. When living in the United States I barely had time to breathe and really take an account of my life. The only thing that I celebrated was my birthday and my children's birthdays. Life moved at a rapid pace in the United States. There was no time to meditate—at least that's what I had been telling myself. However, I still found the time to shop online, attend a party or two, and go on a few dates. I realize that people make time to live how they want to live, although I don't think some people understand what it means to live.

Living is about truly understanding and appreciating God's mercy, grace, and favor. Life is about understanding and knowing who you are as a person. As a mother, I want my children to know who they are and be confidant in who they are. If they don't like who they are, then do something about it. So many times, people live life doing things that they don't want to do to appease someone else. An individual cannot live life trying to please other people. They will go crazy and end up in a state of depression, have emotional breakdowns, and eventually go into a place of isolation.

Living and working in Al Ain allowed me the opportunity to take a break from the fast pace of life. I had time to just come home and sit down and rest my loins. It allowed me to truly listen to Chelsea and hear what her thoughts are on life and about being the only black girl in her class from the United States. It was quite interesting to see she still enjoyed school in this predominately Muslim country. She liked having classmates from New Zealand, South Africa, Syria, Egypt, Jordan, and other parts of the world she had never heard of. Yes, she never heard of Jordan because in the states it wasn't a part of our regular conversation and she was only in sixth grade, so her education of world history was limited. Any parts of the world I had been introduced to during my schooling had long been forgotten.

She and I had social studies lessons together. We would look at the map together to try to find the different countries on the map. We would be surprised to see how close some of the countries were to the United Arab Emirates. We really were living in the middle of the world. Chelsea had fallen in love with maps and researching other countries. She found a love in geography. She would even quiz me.

"Mommy which country has the most pyramids?" Naturally, I would say Egypt because that's what I had been taught that Egypt was the only country with pyramids. She kindly corrected me, "Nope, it's Sudan!" I had to Google to find out if she was right. I guess I'm not smarter than a sixth grader. I remember she and my line sister debating about the exact location of Seychelles. Needless to say, she was right again. Her appetite to explore and learn about other parts of the world were increasing and I couldn't have been more pleased. I was excited about the fact that she wanted to explore the world and didn't mind doing it with me or alone. She has said on numerous occasions that she wants to live in the United Kingdom, mainly because she wants to speak with an English accent. I never tell her that's a silly reason because

I don't want to crush her love of exploration or living in other parts of the world. Also, if that's why she wants to live in a country to speak their dialect, then, do it! If she is living her life the way she wants to, I'm happy for her.

So many times, parents push their kids into doing something that pleases them as a parent instead of supporting the child into becoming what they want to do in life. When I was growing up my mother always would tell my siblings and me, "You have to go at 18 years old." Which meant she was done raising you and you were now on your own. She began telling us that as early as 10 years old. My siblings that were older than I was were taught how to wash clothes, cut up a whole chicken and fry it, and how to catch a public bus across town to pay the light bill. I still don't see how my oldest sister Rita caught the bus miles across town without being kidnapped, but she got it down. My mother refused to raise kids that didn't know how to be independent. I still remember to this day my sister who was about 15 at the time arguing over how to cut up a whole chicken. My mother said, "I'm going to show you one more time how to cut up this damn chicken and it better be done next time or I'm putting you out!" My mother never showed my sister how to cut up a chicken again, and we still had chicken at least once a week cooked by my sister. I don't think my mother would've put my sister out the house, but my sister wasn't going to test it either.

I raise Chelsea a lot like how my mother raised me—to be independent. Chelsea can wash her own clothes, cook breakfast, lunch, and dinner, and clean a house. Some swim parents were really impressed with Chelsea. Chelsea was about 8 years old and after swim practice, she would take a shower, lotion her body, and get dressed by herself while I waited outside. She didn't need any help from me. She is very proud to be able to do things on her own. She was able to bake a cake from the box on her own without any of my help. It's okay to help your kids with various tasks, but they need to know what it feels like to have to work hard for something on their own. Also, it's important to teach children how to advocate for themselves. Chelsea was complaining about one of her teachers taking points off for something she did. She didn't think that was fair because it was unrelated to the work itself. I believe the teacher told her that she was going to take points off for Chelsea talking or something like that. I would normally speak to the teacher educator to educator, but I told Chelsea that she was old enough to advocate on her own behalf with the teachers in a respectable manner. She and I role played how she needed to speak with the teachers and how to express her concerns. I'm not sure if she got the points back or if the teacher even followed through with taking the points; however, she is aware how to advocate for herself in a respectful manner. Chelsea really thrived and matured in the Middle East.

The move had fostered Chelsea's growth and development. She learned personal communication skills that she will use throughout her life.

CHAPTER 8

WELCOME TO INDIA

Chelsea and I traveled to India in the month of November. This was during wedding season in India. I mainly wanted to go to India to visit the Taj Mahal, one of the great wonders of the world. Prior to visiting India, you must obtain a visa. Unlike the visit to Jordan, you can't get a visa at the airport in India. Prior to purchasing our flight to India, I applied for our visas online. I had to be sure I had everything correct, as any wrong information would result in paying again for the application. I've heard that has happened to people. It took about a week to receive our visas. The approval letters were sent to my email. I made sure I printed them immediately and put them in my luggage so I wouldn't forget them. I expected India to be one of the most beautiful countries in the world.

When we arrived at the Delhi International Airport at about 6 o'clock in the morning, our driver was waiting on us holding up a sign with my name on it. I had arranged for a tour company to take us from Delhi to Agra to visit the Taj Mahal, Agra Fort, and some other sites. The driver was Indian and spoke fluent English. He offered us water and asked if we needed anything. He picked us up in a small SUV to drive us from New Delhi to Agra, which was a three-hour drive. Chelsea and I were both still sleepy, so we slept most of the way. Luckily before we doze off for a bit, we were able to catch some of the countryside scenery. There were fields and fields of grasslands and trees, which brought a welcoming feeling of peace and home because we had become accustomed to seeing mostly sand dunes in UAE.

As we got closer into the city part of Agra, the traffic increased tremendously. I had never seen so much traffic piled up in one small area in my life. There were no traffic lanes, so it was like all the defensive drivers created their own lanes in both directions. Chelsea's little face was glued to the car window. Her eyes widened as the mopeds zoomed past the car. Quickly upon seeing this, I became very nervous as our driver dodged in and out of the imaginary lanes. I yelled out one time when a car came in our lane from the opposite direction and quickly switched back into his lane as he passed a vehicle in front of us. I heard the traffic in India was bad, but I didn't expect it to be dangerously bad! It was like all the drivers knew what they were doing, and it was organized vehicle chaos. In addition to the traffic, the large buffalos made a parking space on the sidewalks.

The driver of the tour company was kind enough to take us to our hotel to shower and change. He said that he would return in a couple of hours. Two hours later, he picked us up with our tour guide, Raj. We stayed at the Doubletree Hotel in Agra for one night and one night at the Hilton Garden Inn in New Delhi. Both hotels were reasonably priced, neat, and clean. The Doubletree was nestled into a bricked old business community, not far from the Taj Mahal.

Before making our way to visit the Taj Mahal, the driver took us to an Indian restaurant named Golden Street Restaurant. The restaurant was empty. It looked like they may have been closed, but Raj spoke to someone, and Chelsea and I were escorted to a table. I liked flavorful Indian food, and Chelsea had never really had authentic Indian food in the United States. So, having authentic Indian food for the first time was an experience for her. We both ordered something that we were familiar with, curry chicken and rice. The curry chicken was by far the most flavorful Indian dish I ever had. The chicken was tender and seemed to melt in my mouth and the curry flavor just danced on my tongue. Chelsea and I absolutely loved the chicken curry dish so much that we cleaned our plates, meaning there was no food left over. I paid for our meal with Indian rupees. Prior to traveling outside of

UAE, I would always do the currency exchange at the local Lulu's Market in Al Ain in UAE.

The Taj Mahal

After leaving the restaurant, we made our way through the overly congested traffic to the Taj Mahal. On the way, we saw quite a few buffaloes hanging out on the sidewalk as if they were home. I guess that was home for them. We were the ones not used to seeing buffaloes laying down on the sidewalk and people walking around them. A few loose dogs roamed the streets. The buildings looked dingy and some seemed on the edge of dilapidation. However, business was being conducted as if it was a normal day. I guess it was normal for them, but different for us. We got accustomed to things being quiet on Fridays, which, in the United Arab Emirates, is considered a holy day. But, in India business was conducted like a normal day similar to home in the United States. We really missed being home in the United States, so to hear the tour guide say the work week was Monday through Friday warmed our hearts. At hearing this, Chelsea and I simultaneously looked at each other and smiled. We had never been away from the United States that long. It had been four months since we touched American soil and our hearts were growing weary. We missed home and more importantly, we both missed Rylan. Chelsea missed her dad. We both were getting tired of the video chats, and we needed to hug our family. Every trip we took, she and I would both say, "I wish Rylan was here."

As a mother, you want both all of your children to have the same amazing experiences. However, it was not in my control. Being away from my son was heartbreaking at times. One night I was up late—as I was most nights—watching television when my U.S. phone rang. It was about two in the morning in the UAE but five in the evening in Georgia. I saw Rylan's school on the caller ID, so I immediately answered the phone. It was one of the afterschool teachers talking about Rylan's behavior. I asked to speak to my son. I asked Rylan what the problem was and reminded him about our behavior expectations. My son began teared up into a cry that seemed to have come from the pit of his stomach. Then tears began to fall from my eyes because I knew he missed his mother and he needed me. I missed him just as much and needed to see if my son was truly okay. I reminded him that Chelsea and I would be home for the Christmas break in a couple more weeks and that I loved him. During my talk with him, I wondered if people in the military felt the same way when they are deployed for months or even years at a time.

I wanted to skip town so badly and just run to be with my son, but I couldn't show my daughter that I was a quitter. I was caught between conflicting parenting need of two kids. She was watching my every move, though I sensed she took on those same feelings. It was like we could tell when homesickness was kicking in for the both of us. We would become even closer. She would start sleeping in my bed with me or I would fall asleep watching a YouTube on the computer with her. We were all we had as family then, and our bond was growing ever so tightly.

Viewing the Taj Mahal from a car was impossible. It was nestled in a courtyard surrounded by large red brick gates. We hired one of the photographers standing outside the gate to come in take our pictures by and around the Taj Mahal. As we made our way through the east gate, we received a lot of stares from people. The stares quadrupled the stares we would get in Al Ain. It felt like every other person of different nationalities was staring at us. Many people stopped and asked if we would take pictures with them. It finally got to the point where our tour guide said, "No more pictures." The tour guide explained that many of the Indian people had never seen African-Americans and they were amazed and wanted to capture the moment. Chelsea and I were in complete awe. When you travel to other parts of the world, you can easily take for granted that everyone doesn't have that luxury to be able to travel to other parts of the world.

The Taj Mahal was a spectacular building from the outside. It had four large pillars that stood in each corner of the building. I will admit that I thought the Taj Mahal was a Mosque. Well, it's not a Mosque. Don't criticize me; I don't remember all the history lessons on India and its Taj Mahal.

Chelsea was learning about Asia in school during the time of our visit, so she was very intrigued. Our tour guide, Raj, gave a very detailed lesson on the Taj Mahal. The entire structure of the Taj Mahal is made of white marble stone. The Taj Mahal was built in memory of the wife of Mughal Emperor Shah Jahan. After having their 14th child, the Emperor's wife Mumtaz Mahal became very ill. She asked the emperor to promise her three things after her death. The first thing was that he would not get remarry, he would not have any more children, and that he would build something in her honor. As a result, the Taj Mahal was built in her honor. The Taj Mahal means, "Crown Palace." It took 22 years to complete the structure.

Chelsea, Raj, and I walked up a couple flights of stairs where we were given coverings to put over our shoes. You are not allowed to walk on the marble with your shoes on. There were crowds of people bumping into one another as we made our way down a narrow path inside the monument, the inside of which was dark. The only electricity in the building was one light that hung in the center of the building above the tombs. The structure had beautiful flowers made of precious gem stones of different colors engraved inside and outside. The flowers looked hand-painted. Various parts of the world contributed shipments of marble and gem stones to India to help build the Taj Mahal. Once inside, we were able to walk around the two tombs that house the remains of the Mumtaz

Mahal and Mughal Emperor Shah Jahan. The wife's tomb is in the center while the emperor's is off to the side. The emperor had planned to build the black Taj Mahal and be placed there, but his plans did not go over well with others. The intricate beauty of the Taj Mahal is remarkable, and the love story is even more endearing. The emperor could view the Taj Mahal from his bedroom at Agra Fort, where he eventually died of heartbreak.

We visited Humyans Tomb, Lotus Temple, Agra Fort, the Indian Gate, and the Ghandi Museum. We really turned our India adventure into a history lesson. The Indian people's English was well articulated compared to other countries we visited. I didn't feel there was a language barrier at all. Visiting the Ghandi museum was perfect timing because when we first arrived in the UAE, Chelsea and I watched the Ghandi movie in the hotel. So, we had some background information about Ghandi's work. Chelsea and I enjoyed reading some of Ghandi's words that were posted all over the museum. We were able to walk down the same path he walked before he was killed.

This trip to India made me realize that there is a whole world that exists and that I must explore it more. As I spoke with the native people of India and Jordan, I discovered they were not impressed or pleased with their government. They felt like the government was getting rich off the backs of the poor and that it was difficult to move up in a different income level and prosper financially.

I could really appreciate some of the aspects of the United States government. I felt that if you truly worked hard and believed in yourself, you could make a good living for yourself and your family in the United States and move up income levels. I'm partially addicted to social media and I've seen so many people share their experiences of moving up the income ladder from multi-level marketing to becoming an entrepreneur. Success is as it relates to income and living our best life is very possible in the United States. However, one must take time to really get to know themselves and what it is they want out of life. Many of the citizens from other countries that worked low paying jobs felt that their country doesn't allow its citizens to increase their wealth. Which is why a lot of them have opted to work in different countries to earn more money. We met people and interacted with people from other countries on a regular basis. A Nigerian girl named Cynthia braided Chelsea and I hair sent money home Nigeria so her son could attend private school. She really missed her son as much as I missed Rylan. Our boys were both in grade school.

Contrarily, a lot of the people we met living in the United Arab Emirates that were from other countries outside of the U.S. did not believe their government allowed its citizens to cross into higher income brackets. Many of them were cleaners, nannies, or non-skilled workers. Their pay ranged from 1000 to 1500 AED a month. That equals 270 to 400 USD. Sometimes they must pay for housing out of their salary. Often, they have no other choice but to pick up odd jobs to make ends meet. Their odd jobs may consist of babysitting, cleaning homes, cleaning cars, hanging curtains, and doing small carpenter jobs. I've seen people give money to street workers they drive by because of the pity they have for these dear workers that are picking up trash off the street. Sometimes, I asked some of the workers whether they like it in the UAE. I received mixed reviews. Some loved it there and others didn't for various reasons, including their low, low wages from which they could not escape. As a well-paid foreign worker in UAE I didn't think it was fair for some of the expats to get paid at such a low rate. People were paid based on their nationality, not the job. I always gave the housekeeper more money than the rate she quoted me to clean.

Agra Fort

Agra Fort was our next stop in India after leaving the Taj Mahal. Agra Fort was the home of the emperors of the Mughal Dynasty until 1638. It was hard to believe that India was one of the richest countries in the world. The Agra Fort was made using red sandstone. Some of the original markings of gem stone art are still present. As I said, Agra Fort was the home to many dynasties. It was also the battle grounds of those that tried to conquer the dynasty. The tour guide shared his disgust with the British taking over. It seemed that every country we visited in Asia, the British always tried to conquer or had conquered in some way. I was starting to feel more of a dislike for the British. I wondered if Chelsea picked up on that fact that the British really wanted to conquer the world.

Agra Fort is a unique structure that underwent many changes depending on who was in control. After all the changes in power and battles, it was amazing to see the walls that separated the rooms. We were able to see the Taj Mahal from one of the bedrooms that belonged to the former emperor. The tour guide shared that there were many secret tunnels that were built underground within the fort. One of the shocking things that we saw at Agra Fort were the free monkeys that roamed the fort. There were several monkeys playing with each other while hanging out in the very nearby trees. At first, Chelsea and I were scared, but we played it cool like the other visitors and began taking pictures of the playful animals.

The architecture of the fort was unique. The tour guide shared that the royal rooms were built in so that they would remain cool throughout the year. Luckily, we visited during the month of November so weather in India was very nice and tolerable. At night there was a nice warm breeze and only a small amount of humidity. However, it wasn't desert hot like UAE. There are other parts of India that I would like to visit that I heard were nice.

In the midst of the large crowds of Indians conducting business throughout the day, I felt a sense of peace and tranquility. We were treated with respect and kindness everywhere we visited. This journey of living and traveling in the Middle East was finally giving inner peace. India brought me inner peace and self-forgiveness.

CHAPTER 9

WELCOME TO SRI LANKA

Sri Lanka is an island south of India. Chelsea had no idea we were going. She had heard about Sri Lanka during her world history studies and in conversations by a couple of our friends in UAE that had visited. She thought we were going to Abu Dhabi City for the weekend. I told her to make sure she packed a swimsuit for the weekend. She loved to swim. I couldn't wait to see how she responded once she saw the Indian Ocean.

It was so hard keeping it from her. I really wanted her to be surprised and happy at the same time. I enjoyed surprises and surprising people. So, on Thursday afternoon, I checked her out of school early. We were in our white Nissan Sunny which resembled every other rental car in UAE. The people of UAE *loved* the color white, especially white cars. I literally had to press the panic button on the car remote to find my car because there were so many white cars in the parking lots. This was nothing like living in the United States. Seeing the color white everywhere was becoming more and more irritated and reminded me of how much I missed the United States. I never got used to seeing so many white cars. Nor did I get used to the amount of sand that was tracked into our car and house. I didn't think we needed a vacuum because our villa was all ceramic tiles. The housekeeper had to use a vacuum on our tiled floors to get all of the sand.

On the drive home to meet the driver to take us to the airport, I told her we weren't going to Abu Dhabi for the weekend. She had a look of sadness like *why the hell did you check me out of school early*? Then I yelled out, "We are headed to Sri Lanka, baby!" She looked at me, "Mom, stop playing!" Then I repeated myself. "We are headed to Sri Lanka, Colombo. We only have a few minutes before the driver takes us to the airport, so hurry up!" She finally gave a smile and then a facial expression that said, *she got me again*. Playing jokes on each other was becoming a real joy for us.

It sounds like we were living a life of luxury with a driver to take us to the airport. It wasn't luxury. It was cheaper and more efficient. Driving to Dubai International Airport can be a hassle if you don't know where you're going. There are three different terminals located in three different locations not next to each other. Each terminal had different airlines. I was clueless about any of them. On top of that, the cost to park your car at the airport was dang near the price of the rental car. I learned that from a friend when she and her husband parked at the airport for the weekend and their bill was 300 USD. The price of the driver was half that and I didn't have to worry about driving home after a mini vacation.

Following a recommendation, I arranged for a driver for the weekend in Sri Lanka. I never heard of Sri Lanka until I moved to the Middle East. Sri Lanka is an island country located south of India in the Indian Ocean. The population of Sri Lanka was about 21 million and the size of West Virginia. The capital is Colombo and we landed there in the wee hours of the morning. It was still dark outside. The driver served as our tour guide and chauffeur for the weekend. Our driver was a native of Sri Lanka and knew the city and outskirts very well. He looked like he could have been Indian, but he wasn't Indian. He reminded me of the character He suggested we explore Kandy and then make our way to Galle which was on coast. The problem was I hadn't booked a hotel in Kandy. The driver drove us from the airport to the Kandy area which was about an hour away. I thought the traffic was bad in India, but Sri Lanka gave the traffic in India a run for its money. Kandy was in the mountains of Colombo. The driver sped through twists and turns up steep narrow lanes in the mountains, causing me to pray silently as Chelsea laid her head on my lap. Yes, I was scared as hell. I didn't want to die in the mountains of Colombo in an accident. The driver stopped at one hotel that was built inside the mountains. He got out the car with a promise that he would be right back. He was checking to see if there were any rooms available for us. It was so early in the morning we would only need a room for a few hours to get a couple hours of sleep and a shower. Unfortunately, they were booked. After the third hotel, the driver decided to take us to one of his friend's bed and breakfast. To get to there, he had to drive up a very steep narrow hill surrounded by trees. It was completely dark with only the headlights from the car to give us light. I dared not to look over the edge, so I looked out which I saw nothing because it was pitch black. All I could do was pray. Here I was with my baby girl in Kandy, Colombo in the middle of nowhere with a man I just met going to a bed and breakfast that was not registered as a business. This was because I didn't make the proper reservations that was aligned with our arrival time.

An old man that looked like he was in his mid-sixties ushered Chelsea and me to a room that had a bed and bathroom and a large window that showed the view of a forestry lake in the back of the house. The bed was surrounded by a large net to keep out flying insects. Chelsea gave me a disturbed look. I knew then that I had to remain calm because if I acted nervous, then she would become nervous. So, I played it cool. "We will only be here for a couple of hours and we are out of here," I said with definitiveness. However, I was just as nervous as she was. At that moment no one in the world knew where I was or who I was with. I told my friends we were going to Sri Lanka, but I didn't give them the driver's name or contact information. That night, I vowed to always give the information of the driver and hotel to my close family and friends. Chelsea was still a little nervous and so was I, so I downloaded the night light app on my phone, and we slept in the creaky full-size bed hugged up with the nightlight on for the first time in our lives.

The next morning, we washed up in the old white bathroom connected to the room. There were a couple of spiders creeping in the corners. I said, "If you don't bother me, I won't bother you" as I washed my face. I was happy to have hot running water coming from the faucet and soap. I always traveled with my own Dove soap and face towels. Nevertheless, the old man gave us towels to use. After we got dressed, we opened the door to the room where we could see that we were at someone's two-bedroom home. The old man introduced his son and dog to us. The dog was an old shabby looking dog that stood nearly to my thigh and he looked like he was living in his last days. When Chelsea saw the dog she quickly walked to the driver's car and hopped inside. The driver miraculously showed up out of nowhere. I think he slept in the car or on a nearby couch. I couldn't quite detect where he came from and it didn't matter. It was daylight and sightseeing places were opening soon. I quickly hopped in the car with Chelsea and our bags. The man was standing outside the car for some time talking to the driver and then it dawned on me that I needed to compensate the man for allowing us to sleep at his home for a few hours. So, I grabbed a couple thousand Sri Lankan rupees and passed it to the old man and thanked him again for his hospitality. That sounds like a lot of money, it was equivalent to 13 USD. The man appeared to be pleased with the compensation.

Our first sight was the Temple of the Sacred Tooth Relic. The temple is in the Royal Complex in Kandy. As we approached the entry into the complex, we paid a street vendor a couple rupee to rent scarves to cover our legs. Chelsea and I both had on shorts which was not acceptable to wear inside the temple. Women must have their legs covered to the knee. I was not surprised because the same rules apply for entering a mosque. In addition, we had to remove our shoes. I was happy to have worn socks that day. There were hundreds of people that appeared to be locals and foreigners. Chelsea and I received stares from many people that were visiting the temple. People had small bowls of flowers to make as an offering to the relic. The temple is significant because it holds a tooth of the Buddha. The temple is white, and we had to take a couple twist and turns as we got a glimpse. We walked through the small elaborate tunnel that had stairs and a beautifully painted ceiling which led to the inner chamber. The sacred tooth shrine is at the upper level of the inner shrine. The tunnel was dimly lit with only light coming from the outside at the tunnel opening. On the lower level of the inner shrine, there were drummers dressed in fabric and head dress played music and drums. The sacred tooth relic is located inside the chamber at the center (inside the brazen door). The golden casket that contains the sacred tooth relic is enveloped by seven caskets of precious metal which we were able to get a glimpse. At the lower level of the temple were many different Buddha statues. There was even a printed story of the Buddha on the wall above our head. Chelsea and I were in awe of the golden Buddha statue located in the new shrine hall. We slowly read the story of how the Buddha was born and the practice of Buddhism. Sri Lankan people practice Buddhism. Chelsea and I really enjoyed reading about the Buddha. Chelsea was soaking up all the culture of the Sri Lankans and so was I. She starred at the Buddhas with intense eyes. I could see her mind drifting off into another world. I didn't interrupt her stares. She would read the inscriptions.

"Mommy why are they putting things by the Buddha?" She was intrigued by people coming into the temple to place flowers on the altar as they said a silent prayer on bended knees. On our way back to the car, we were able to get pictures with statues of Prince Dantha and Princess

Hemamala who brought the Tooth Relic to Sri Lanka in the 4th Century AD.

After leaving the temple, Chelsea and I had walked a little taller and more confidant like, "Yes! We are smarter now that we've visited the Sacred Tooth Relic and read the birth of the Buddha." If you asked us a day later about the birth of the Buddha, we probably would have remembered only bits and pieces. During our visit, Chelsea said, "I wish Rylan was here." That was becoming a common saying experiencing something new. I looked in her big brown eyes that now sparkled from new knowledge and said, "Me, too, baby girl, me, too." Even though we enjoyed our travels and learning about the culture of other countries, we still wanted Rylan to share these moments with us.

The people of Sri Lanka were very gracious and treated us with respect and care. They welcomed us with a warm smile at each establishment we visited. Their English wasn't too bad. People always asked where we were from. Once we said America, it seemed like they preferred American dollars over Sri Lankan Rupees. We had no dollars to give. We had dirhams which they turned down when we offered to pay for anything in dirhams. Dirhams were not wanted or welcomed in Sri Lanka. Thank goodness I did the currency exchange before I left UAE.

I hoped Chelsea was learning about staying committed to a task or an assignment. It was a definite struggle being away from my son. Missing his seventh birthday sent me into a moment of depression. I was supposed to attend two different events that weekend, but all I could get myself to do was run the neighborhood and lie in bed. All I could think about was what mother misses her son's seventh birthday. I would've loved to fly home and surprise him, but that meant I would've missed workdays without pay and I would've had to buy two plane tickets. I couldn't go to the U.S. and leave my daughter in the UAE. That would've cost a minimum of three thousand U.S. dollars for just a few days. I had a financial goal and spending money like that would take me off course. I asked my ex-husband if he could come with my girlfriend who is also Rylan's Godmother to visit us during his summer break. I agreed to purchase the ticket and when I got out for the summer, Chelsea and I would bring him home. Right before I was about to purchase the plane ticket, he said Rylan couldn't come because it was too far. I was so disappointed and felt defeated. I really started questioning my motherhood. I dealt with a major internal conflict. One side of me would say, "You don't know what they are saying! What kind of mother leaves their son behind to frolic around the world? This is a great experience for Chelsea. She is really maturing and growing a love for exploration." The conflict was becoming so bad that I called to Atlanta to have a counseling session over the phone with my therapist. He reminded me, "That was the only decision you could make at that particular time."

There were many days when I was at work and the teachers and principal were carrying out a full-blown conversation in Arabic. I didn't understand a word they were saying. I constantly asked God, "Why am I here?" I always felt that I was put in a position to help children, teachers, parents, and administration or all of them. However, I was at a lost as to which group I was supposed to help when I didn't speak their primary language. Finally, God answered. "You are not here for someone else. You are here for you." For once in my life, I was in a position in which I had the time and energy to work on me. I had the time to sit down and meditate and think about all the decisions I made prior to moving to the middle east. I thought about why I got married, and why I had children. I felt like those were two major decisions that altered my life forever. As Chelsea would talk about the many different things she wanted to be as an adult, I questioned what happened to all the things I wanted to be in life. Why didn't I follow through with becoming a choreographer or becoming a journalist or news reporter? I wanted to be a host for *Teen Summit* on BET. Then I wanted to be a news beat reporter? Then finally, I wanted to be a talk show host. I have only myself to blame for I didn't become those things. However, I wish I had parents that fostered my dreams and aspirations instead of their goals and dreams for me. By and large, though, they instilled values that allowed me to live a healthy life and become a productive citizen in our society.

I want to be the parent who exposes her children to different parts of the world and different cultures and allow them to decide for themselves how they want to live their life. Therefore, I don't say anything negative to Chelsea when she states she wants to be a major YouTuber and have her own fashion company. You never know what God has in store.

After leaving the Temple of the Sacred Tooth Relic in Kandy, we toured an herbal plant plantation that made medicines and creams. Susantha Spice and Herbal Garden was quite unique. Believe it or not, most medicines come from plants, those that are legal and illegal. We were greeted by one of the associates at the plantation that took us on a tour of each plant. There were all different kinds of plants. The sales associate explained each plant and what is was used for. We were able to smell and even taste some of the pure plant products. At the end, we were taken inside the store where we could purchase some of the products. Some of the products included sandalwood oil and cream which is a natural cosmetic beauty care product. It helps with wrinkles and fine lines. Then the cinnamon oil which they stated was good for shivering cold, tooth pain, ear pain, and mouth swelling. The herbal tooth powder is used to ensure strong white teeth, healthy gums, fresh breath, and stops tooth decay. The green oil is highly effective against migraine headaches, sinusitis, and hangovers. The turmeric skin bleach fairness cream is used to take away scars, leaving the skin a lighter shade. They sole 24 different products that were made from plants. I purchased the sandalwood creams and red oil with herbal balm (siddartha oil). According to the associate, the Red Oil with Herbal Balm is used to help arthritis, gout, joint pains, and muscular pains. Since I started exercising, I noticed my joints were starting to ache. Many of the expats thought we lacked vitamin D. My day allowed me to have more time to exercise. I didn't feel so drained after work. My weight was the highest it had ever been at 200 pounds. I wanted to feel better and look better. I joined Weight Watchers and started exercising daily. I walked and ran 3 miles a day. Chelsea was excited to join me at times. They had medicines for all kinds of problems from menstrual cramps to diabetes. These were all-natural products.

Our second hotel was one of the nicest hotels that we stayed in during our travel. We stayed at the Lavanga Resort and Spa located in the Galle area. The hotel was very nice, and our room had a beautiful view of the pool and Indian Ocean. We arrived at the hotel at night, so it was hard to take in the beauty of nature. However, the next day, the sunlight reflected the ocean and radiated through our hotel room and woke us up. I got out the bed first and looked out the window. Right beneath us was a rectangular shaped pool with blue tiles which made the water look even more like a royal sparkling blue. There were palm trees that stood around the pool and just below that were cabanas resting in the sand that led to the beach and the Indian Ocean. Chelsea and I swam in the Indian Ocean which was totally different than lounging in the Dead Sea. Chelsea was much more vibrant and active in the Indian Ocean. She danced in the ocean and play around with her shadow on the beach. In the Dead Sea she moved like a blind man trying to find his way. The sea was rocky and slippery. She had a small cut on her leg that made for a bad sting as she wobbled and tiptoed around the Dead Sea. The scene looked like something you saw on a postcard. I whispered, "Thank you, God." I had to give thanks because I couldn't believe that this little girl from Detroit, Michigan was looking out at the Indian Ocean.

I remember being in fourth grade and my teacher Ms. Devise would call someone to go to the front of the room and identify the four oceans on the huge world map that she pulled down from the top of the chalk board. I remember walking to the front of the room and using the pointer to say as I pointed to each one, "Pacific Ocean, Atlantic Ocean, Indian Ocean, and Arctic Ocean." I never thought in my wildest dreams that I would see and swim in the Indian Ocean. I saw the Atlantic Ocean before when I was a teenager and my dad allowed me to go to the Jersey Shore with some friends. There I saw the Atlantic Ocean. My kids and I were able to swim in the Atlantic Ocean after Chelsea's swim meet. Also, when Chelsea was in first grade she and I took a trip to California where we went swimming in the Pacific Ocean. The only ocean to visit now is the Arctic Ocean.

The more we traveled, the more I started to see Chelsea changing. She spoke differently about traveling. She was not afraid to travel anywhere. If I said, "We are headed to Mars" she would start packing a suitcase. Every trip was like an exploration and adventure. Although our trip to Sri Lanka started off a little scary, it was ending with confidence.

Visiting Sri Lanka was a trip Chelsea, and I will cherish. It allowed us to experience things we've never done like swimming in the Indian Ocean, seeing how cinnamon is taken from a cinnamon tree and used to produce cinnamon oil and cinnamon powder. Our bond became tighter and tighter. She opened up more and more to me about her feelings about school and being the only black girl and only American on her swim team. She was comfortable in who she was as a girl and as a young black girl. As a female raising a daughter, I hope and pray that she doesn't try to take on the images she sees on magazine covers, television commercials, and social media. I want her to be comfortable and confidant in her skin complexion, with her body, her hair, her dialect, and personality. Chelsea spoke more about places she would like to travel. She even mentioned going to college abroad.

This experience had her thinking about living and visiting geographical places I had never heard about until moving to the Middle East.

Dating

Even though I was getting more looks from men, I was not interested in dating. I really had no desire or the energy to date or take time getting to know someone who I may not see after the end of my work contract. Everyone did not feel this way. There were some instant hook-ups. There were people who became couples within two weeks of arriving in UAE and meeting each other. It really wasn't that hard to fall madly in love with someone in Al Ain because it was a very small place and there wasn't much to do there. If you wanted adventure and a good party, you had to make your way to Abu Dhabi or Dubai. I realized that once I attended a couple of parties in Dubai, there seemed to be more men looking to mingle. The parties were filled with nothing but expats. Some people used the dating sites to meet people, and some met them through social media. There were a few guys that sent me messages via Facebook Messenger trying to hook up, but I just wasn't interested. I was in no shape to deal with the foolishness that goes along with dating. I was finally free from a broken 14-year marriage and all the crazy mini relationships I got involved in after my failed marriage.

Back in the U.S. I met this one guy at a house party. We spent a lot of time talking on the phone, going out to parties, and hanging out playing all kinds of games. After a couple of months of dating, I found out he was married. I know you're wondering why I didn't know he was married. Well, in Atlanta a lot of married men were great at keeping their marital status concealed. He didn't wear a wedding band, he never posted pictures of his wife on social media, and more importantly when I asked if he was married or involved with anyone, he said, "No." He finally confessed that he was married only because some woman created a fake Facebook page acting like she was me and contacted his wife. So, after he had a conversation with his wife about me, he confessed to me, not knowing that I had no idea that he was married. He thought I was mad at him for going out partying the night before instead of hanging out with me. A few hours later, my brother called me and said my mom passed away. It was April 14, 2016, and my life changed forever. My outlook on life and dating really changed… so I thought.

I didn't get involved with another man for nine months. He was Mr. Opportunist and another liar. We met at a local sports bar. He was 6 feet 4 inches and had light brown caramel skin. He was bald with a light brown beard, which brought him lots of attention. He was a well-groomed, charming man. We went out several times and really enjoyed each other's company. However, I knew something seemed strange when he was acting strange on the weekend of his birthday. I told him that I wanted to take him out for his birthday. However, on the day of his birthday he posted a video on Instagram of him and another girl at a lounge. This was after he told me he was out with his brother and best friend. I should've known something wasn't right. Men don't use the term, "best friend." My gut said, "Something isn't right." I was upset and confronted him about the girl in the video. He lied and said it was a friend from his hometown that happened to be in town with other friends. As it turned out, she was actually his finance that he was living with that put him out after she found out about him cheating on her. He had been cheating on her for years and she was finally fed up. He was a 45-year-old man that still enjoyed dating more than one woman at a time.

So, when the Muslim women on my job asked if the men in the U.S. liked a lot of women, I sadly responded, "Yes." However, the Muslim men like women, too. Why else would they be allowed to have four wives at the same time?

Dating in the UAE seemed just as hard for black women as dating in the USA. It appeared that most of the black men were married or not interested in the black women. This was my experience: The only black or brown men that my friends and I had been approached by have all been from other continents., A few African men came across my Facebook or

Instagram and would send me a DM. It went a little something like this,

"Hello Beautiful."

"Hello."

"How are you today?"

"I'm fine."

"I would love to take you out and get to know you."

"Thank you, but I'm not interested."

"I'm not saying I want to date you. I can be your friend."

"I'm not interested. Thank you and have a nice day."

"You are so beautiful. Do you live in Dubai?"

"No. Al Ain."

"Maybe I can visit you in Al Ain."

"I'm not interested."

"Can I have your number, so we can talk?"

I usually blocked them from contacting me again on Facebook or Instagram after that. It was annoying to have someone you never met constantly send you messages and advances to date me and I wasn't interested. I viewed those men to be very desperate or had an ulterior motive. However, I've heard of some love connections taking place from a girl responding to a guy in her DM. One of my friends thought that I was blocking my blessing because I said I'm not going to meet my boyfriend via DM. She only said that because she met her Pakistan lover from Facebook messenger that pleased her on a regular basis and allowed her to relieve some stress. I was determined that if God wanted me to meet a man, He would not send him via my DM because he knows I would block him. I felt that going on dates for a free meal knowing I had no interest in the guy and having recreational sex was just not me. It was like I was morphing into another person that didn't need all the thrills that dating brought.

There were some love connections and marriages. I met a few people that found a husband or a wife in the UAE. The blending of nationalities has made some beautiful unions. There were also some breakups. It was interesting how some of the women would hold their husband or boyfriend's hand just a little tighter in social settings. I remember there was a pool party and two ladies, and I were talking to a guy we hadn't seen in several months. He had lost a lot of weight. While in the middle of talking to us, his girlfriend walked up to him and turned his head toward her and started talking to him and practically forced his mouth to hers. That was the weirdest feeling. I had never a woman mark her territory in such a way. We all laughed about it and said that she was probably in her 20s. I found out later that she had just turned 30.

There were also some men that just wanted sex and were upfront about it. One day I was driving on a highway leading into the desert. The maximum speed limit was 130 kph. I was driving about 120 kph and a silver 2-door Audi with dark black tinted windows pulled up on the side of me. At first, I thought maybe my Abaya was hanging out the door. I pulled on my Abaya to make sure it was flapping in wind between the door and the car. So, I then sped up and the car catches up to mine again. I was clueless about what was going on. I started to get a little nervous because I'm traveling by myself on a road in the desert in the middle of nowhere. The window finally slides down and an Arab gentleman wearing a bleached crisp white kandura and head wrap is in the driver seat. He had on a pair of aviator sunglasses and sported a jet-black beard. He was quite sexy looking. He asked me to pull over. I was very hesitant, so I looked to see if my gas cap was open. It wasn't open, so I drove a little further. The man then sped up again and asked if I would pull over. I slowly pulled over and he pulled up beside me. He complimented me on my hair. The men there really like the long braids. He went on to ask where I was from and if we could exchange numbers. I gave him my WhatsApp number. I felt it would be safer to give him my WhatsApp number. That way if I wasn't interested, then I could easily block him on the App. We texted via WhatsApp but that presented a huge language barrier. His written English was not good. I didn't even attempt to type in Arabic. Arabic writing looked like scribbles. Our conversations went something like this,

"Your hair is beautiful, and the smile is beautiful."

"Thank you."

"Are you alone at home or with family?"

"I live alone. Do you live with family?"

"Yes, living with parents and family."

"Do you have Snapchat?"

"No. I don't."

The small talk continued for a couple of weeks. After that, he must have gathered up the nerve to ask, "Do you like romance?" I was surprised by the question, but I responded, "Yes." Then he sends me a picture of a black girl with curly wild hair wearing a tightly fitted green bodysuit shaking her large ass with a large butterfly tattoo that stretched over her entire buttocks. The first thing I thought about was *how the hell did he get this video because the government blocks all the sex websites and Rated-R Amazon movies?* However, I responded with, "That is sex, not romance." I eventually blocked him, too. My dating life was not as busy as it was in the U.S. and I was okay with that. I spent a lot of time working on myself and getting over a failed marriage, the death of a parent, and missing my baby boy.

I went on a coffee date with an Egyptian gentleman I met at the grocery store. I was shopping for groceries at Lulu's, the most popular grocery store in the UAE. As I walked down one of the grocery aisles, a man walked past and made eye contact with me. To show off my southern hospitality, I said "hello" and kept minding my business. As I walked to my car, the same man was walked up to my car as I was placing my groceries inside.

"Hello, you're very beautiful," he said.

"Thank you."

"Where are you from? South Africa?" This was the next common line. Most of the people that were not from America thought all the black people in the middle east were from South Africa. It was like they never saw a black person outside of South Africa. Although I rarely met black South Africans. Most of the ones I met were Indian or Caucasian descent. He went on making small talk about where he worked and how long he lived in Al Ain. He was an older gentleman from Egypt. He looked like he was in his late 40s. He had a cleaned shaved hairless face and a delicate smile. He didn't come off aggressive, so I gave him my WhatsApp number. Something about him made me curious and I wanted to know more about him. He sent "Good Morning" messages and flower emojis every day. He asked me out several times before I finally agreed.

Our first date was at LaBrioche, a coffee café style restaurant. That night, I wore a pair of fitted jeans, t-shirt, and a blazer with sandals. I wore my regular clothes outside of work. The dress code for public places was not strictly enforced or frown upon. When I arrived about 10 minutes after the meeting time, he was already there and had ordered a cappuccino. He stood up and gave me an innocent smile that showed his perfectly white teeth. He suggested that we moved to a booth. He insisted that we sit side by side instead of across from each other. I refused and said, "Its best that I sit across from you, so I can see you and not have to turn my head."

He talked about how UAE had changed over the last two years, and the expats were being charged more and more. He wore a silver wedding band that I didn't notice when I first met him.

"Are you married? "I asked.

With hesitation, he slowly responded, "Yes."

"Where is your wife?"

"She in Egypt with kids."

"So how many children do you have?" I asked. I couldn't help thinking these men know they love women. He probably was looking for another wife or someone to have sex with while his wife was in Egypt.

"Three, sixteen, eleven, , and eight," he said as he touched each finger to represent a kid. I then went on to ask if it was okay for him to go out with other women while his wife was in Egypt.

"Yes, it is okay."

I didn't believe that one bit. He mentioned that he was allowed to have four wives. I didn't agree with that law which was created for the benefit of the men. However, men that needed support and had no other options could benefit from being a second or third wife. It was common for men in UAE to have multiple wives. We continued with small talk about our jobs. He kept saying, "I'm feel so happy when I see you." He asked if we could go out again. I said that I would think about it. However, I knew I was not interested in being a second or third wife.

As he walked me to my car, he linked his arm in my arm as if we were walking down an aisle as bride and groom. After walking a few feet, I politely unlocked my arm from his. I thanked him for the coffee date and got into my car. Next thing I knew he hopped into my car. I looked at this man *like what the hell are you doing? The date is over, dude.* He took my hand into his hand and declared, "I feel so happy when I see you." "Can I see you tomorrow?" I said "no." He then kissed my hand after I refused to cheek kiss. He let out a slight laugh when I turned my head indicating that I wasn't okay with cheek kissing him. "I will see you later," I said in a stern voice. He then got out the car and walked away.

Like most women, I would like a healthy, fun, exciting, and loving relationship. I didn't want to be like my mother. She died without a love interest, boyfriend, or husband by her side. Growing up, I witnessed my mother jump in and out of relationships. The longest relationship I'd known her to have was with James. He was a bus driver for the city of Detroit. She and James lived together on the west side of Detroit. They seemed to get along well. They had little arguments every now and then. I remember my mom saying James could be a better father to his sons like he was to his daughters. They were together for several years. He bought my mom jewelry, but never an engagement ring. I learned later that James was still married to his estranged wife. When he retired from the Detroit Department of Transportation, he moved to Alabama. My mother had to move out of his house because the house belonged to James and his estranged wife. His wife wanted the house since James was moving out of the state. I think my mother was hurt, but she managed to never show it.

When my mother was dying, she mentioned that the one regret she had was getting involved with a married man, which was my father. I think she felt that she wasted good years of her life on a man that would never marry her. Even though she had two kids out of the relationship, she would never know what kind of relationship she could have had with someone that wasn't married. My mother had her share of dating which is why she felt like she was an expert at giving dating advice. Any advice she gave about a man was usually right.

After my mother died, I found a note inside her Bible that said, "A loving relationship with a man." She wanted to find a loving relationship with a man, and she knew that God was the only one that could help her. I spent a lot of time praying in the Middle East. I'm not sure if it was due to everyone around me constantly praying or the fact that I knew I needed God to help me get through some of the foolishness that took place in the UAE. I constantly had to pray for patience.

As for how well relationships are developed the Middle East, I sometimes wondered if dating was eliminated and one just jumped right into marriage, would the marriage last longer. I talked to some of the teachers at my school about dating and asked if they never dated someone. Dating for Emiratis is not allowed in their culture. When I ask them if they've ever sneaked to date, they looked at me with big bright eyes and said, "No." Or, they would say "I marry my cousin." I asked if they sneaked and dated because I was told by a gas station attendant that the local Emiratis secretly dated. I walked in the store to get some items when I noticed this Message in a Bottle trinket. It had a small heart and flower attached to it. More than half of the message bottles had been purchased. I said to the attendant, "Who in the world is buying this foolishness?" The Indian attendant leaned over as if he was telling me a secret and said, "Well it's not people like me and you." I wrinkled my face and said, "Well who is it because the locals can't have boyfriends and girlfriends." He looked at me with a face of *are you kidding me*? "They have boyfriends and girlfriends" he said. "Do you see this stuff behind me?" He tilted his head to his left shoulder. Behind him were two glass shelves filled with different kinds of condoms and lubrications. "People like me and you are not buying it," he said in a whisper. They (referencing the locals) buy it.

He went on to say, "Sometimes they use the lubrication to go through the back door, so she can stay a virgin." I was dumbfounded and didn't want to believe him. I didn't want to believe that my Emirati friends would do such a thing. I had been in the UAE for about 4 months. I yelled at him, "Stop telling stories!" He insisted, "Do you see them in the malls on their phone?" "They are hooking up through some app on their phones in the mall." I laughed and walked out the store. Later that evening, I shared what the man said with a friend, and she said that she heard the same thing about people meeting up at the malls through an App on their phones. I found it funny and mysterious. About a week later, I was in the mall, and I saw a group of teenage Muslim boys giggling with their cell phones out while staring and giggling at some teenage girls as they passed by on the escalator. I thought maybe there is a little truth to that rumor.

Sex in the UAE does exist, and some people were having a lot of it, but I wasn't one of them. The teachers and staff members stated that the Sheik highly encourages them to have babies to increase the population. The cost to have a baby in the UAE is very different than the USA. I went to visit a couple that moved to the UAE at the same time I did. They were from the United States. Chelsea and I stopped by their flat (that's what they call apartments here). We were dropping off a gift because they had just had a baby. This was the wife's first pregnancy. She stated that she didn't really feel much because as soon as she mentioned she was in pain, they quickly gave her an epidural and more medication. She remembered having some preeclampsia, and then she woke up to her baby on her chest. She said that her hospital room was like staying in a luxury hotel. She was offered to get her hair, make-up, and her lashes done during her hospital stay. The next day, she and her husband were greeted by a nurse with a credit card machine to settle her bill. They both looked at each other and immediately thought, "Oh my God! We're going to need to take out a loan." But then the nurse said, "Your bill is 500 AED." They gladly and quickly paid the bill. They spent $136 USD for a cesarean delivery to deliver their baby in Abu Dhabi, United Arab Emirates. I paid over 10 times that amount to deliver my son in the United States.

I guess you could say I spent most of my time dating myself and getting to know me more. I took myself out to dinner. Dining alone gave me the opportunity to enjoy my food and watch the interactions of others that may have been on a date. As I watched the married Emirati couples at the restaurant, I thought about how boring their relationship appeared. The husband barely interacted with the wife. The women dressed in all black from head to toe with their face covered didn't show any excitement at the dinner table with their husband or with other female friends. The best date I found during that time was with myself or with my daughter.

CHAPTER 10

WELCOME TO THAILAND

This spring break was like no other Chelsea and I had experienced. Chelsea, my line sister, and I decided to travel to Thailand for spring break which started off horrible. We took an overnight flight that landed us in Thailand on Friday morning about 7 o'clock. My line sister had set up an excursion that morning that required wearing relaxed clothing. When we arrived at the airport in Bangkok, Thailand our bags were not there. We were told that they would be delivered that evening. So, we decided to explore Bangkok by going on an evening bike tour with Grasshopper Tour company. The bike tour started at dusk and the sun was nowhere to be found. I hadn't ridden a bike in about a year and definitely not one at night. Chelsea was just getting used to riding a bike and it was evident as we rode down narrow alleyways and streets. For instance, she ran into a lady at a fruit stand as her bike wobbled through a narrow dark alley, holding on to her helmet that was lit with various lights. We got more light from the street lights and cars speeding by. The tour guide, Golf, was so patient with Chelsea. It took her a minute to get the hang of riding a bike again. She almost bumped her bike into a parked motorcycle on one of the streets. I prayed to God, "Please, God, don't let my baby get hit by a car." I encouraged her to keep trying. "You got this!" "Good job!" I would yell when she would ride for a block without crashing into something. There was a couple with us that eventually linked up with another bike tour group at one of the stops.

That was the first time we had ever ridden bikes together and the first time we did it on a tour. We pedaled through Thammasat University where we then caught a ferry boat across the Chao Phraya River to Wat Arun Ratchawararam, meaning the Temple of Dawn. The temple is named after the Indian God Aruna (God of Dawn). The temple was absolutely stunning. The lights shined on the colorful decorated spires and stands that sparkled and reflected off the nearby river. The grand pagoda (or prang in Thai) at Wat Arun, which is surrounded by four smaller pagodas, has the design features and structure of a Khmer-style pagoda. The 70-meter tall grand pagoda was beautifully decorated with tiny pieces of colored glass and Chinese porcelain placed delicately into intricate patterns. It was one of the most beautiful structures we had seen in our travels. There were many different Buddhas located around the temple. We didn't go inside the temples because it was closed which meant that it was fewer tourists and we could really explore the area more freely. The area of the temple was peaceful and serene. We all took lots of pictures. We even took a group picture striking a meditation pose of the buddha. We laughed at each other trying to perfect the pose just right for a quick photo opportunity.

After our quick photo shoot, we made our way through the world-famous Bangkok flower market. We parked our bikes and walked through the market. The flower market was booming. There were people everywhere putting together flower arrangements for weddings, parades, and other events. People were bagging up flowers and selling flowers. There were all kinds of flowers I had never seen, in all different colors. There was bright yellow, red, pink, green, blue, and purple flowers everywhere. The market smelled like a sea of perfumes. Our tour guide treated us to some street meat (chicken), sticky rice, and fresh fruit. I was hesitant about eating the street food. Chelsea and my line sister loved it and ate all the chicken and fruit. The sticky rice was just like its name, sticky. The rice was stuck together in plastic wrap.

Next, we cycled through some of the busy streets. I became a little nervous for Chelsea, but she had gotten the hang of it and rode close to Golf. I occasionally videotaped the experience since I was in the back of the line. I was really in awe. I had to pinch myself to really take the adventure all in. I looked up in the night sky as if I was talking to my mom, like *can you believe your baby girl from Detroit, Michigan is exploring Bangkok, Thailand with her 11-year-old daughter on a bike?* I whispered, "Thank you, God. Thank you, Momma."

After the flower market, we cycled our way to the Wat Pho which is home to the reclining Buddha. We couldn't see the reclining Buddha, but we were able to take in the decorative, quiet, peaceful temple grounds. As usual, we took pictures of the different Buddha and small temples. There were beautifully illuminated chedi spires covered in porcelain mosaics. It was almost like having a privileged tour. I felt like a celebrity with an all access pass and private tour. Finally, we biked past the Grand Palace to Sanam Luang where we could see the sparkling chedis of the palace. This was one of the best tours that I had experienced. It started off shaky, but once we got the hang of riding a bike, we were good to go. Chelsea really enjoyed the bike tour. She and I were both very proud of her for sticking with it and not giving up on the bike riding. She realized that she could do it if she just stuck with it.

After spending a couple of days in Bangkok, Chelsea and I flew to Phuket without our bags. We had to buy new clothes because we found out that our bag was sent to Manchester,

United Kingdom instead of Bangkok, Thailand. The airline stated that it would be a couple days before we got our bag and that they would send it to Phuket once it arrived. I was beyond mad. I wrote a letter to every department of that airline. A supervisor was waiting for us with cash in his hands to pay us as we checked in to return to Dubai. However, our trip to Phuket made up for the lack of luggage and the botched floating market trip in Bangkok. Yes, I said botched floating market trip.

We decided to take a trip to the floating market. A street police officer in Bangkok called a taxi driver to take us to the floating market. We didn't know the floating market was over an hour away and by the time we got there, there was only an hour and half left before the market closed. However, the taxi driver knew and the associates selling the ticket to the market knew, but no one told us. So, as we boarded the boat to take us to through the floating market, we noticed a lot of the stores were closed. We told the boat driver to take us back to the area where he picked us up. He then decided to take us to another area 45 minutes away. My line sister and I began shouting at the boat driver to take us back. By this time, it was pitch dark and he had to use a flash light to steer us through the muddy murky swap water. We passed homes that sat on the dirty water. There were people taking baths in the water, fishing in the water, and kids playing in the water. We yelled at the driver numerous times, "Take us back!"

"Take us back!" He said okay but would then drive out further. We were so pissed. By the time we made it back, the person that sold us the ticket was gone. The only people there was the taxi driver and family. We demanded our money back or we were going to call the police. The taxi driver kept saying, "Let's go. We need to leave." The man of the family who was probably the owner refused to give us our money back. He jumped in his truck and almost ran me over as I tried to take a picture of his license plate. We finally got into the car with the taxi driver for the long hour commute home. We asked him why he took us if he knew they were closing. He didn't respond. He acted like he didn't understand our question. That may have been the case. The people in Thailand had the worst English out of all the countries we had visited.

I was surprised to learn that the people who worked in the high tourist areas really struggled with English. As Trevor Noah said in his book, "English is the language of the world and money" (Born a Crime: Stories from a South African Childhood, 2016). When we went to a restaurant in Phuket and Chelsea asked about the chicken that was on the menu. The waiter didn't understand the question. So, we asked, "Are they chicken wings?" He said, "No" and put his hand over his heart. I then asked, "Chicken heart?" The waiter walked away and came back with a raw chicken breast in a bowl. We all said at the same time, "Chicken breast." He didn't know the English word "breast." I realized that poor countries lacked educating their people the English language. I asked one of the hotel clerks how he learned to speak English. He explained that he learned to speak English from watching television and music. American music can be heard all over the world. I was shocked the first time I heard American music in the mall. The hip hop music was playing with all the curse words. I was in complete shock. I thought wait, *I thought you weren't allowed to use profanity in this country. Maybe you just can't say, "Fuck you."*

We spent our last few days in Thailand exploring the islands and taking excursions. We really enjoyed going to Tiger Kingdom in Phuket. The Tiger Kingdom is a place that allows you to get up close to the tigers. Deirdre and I paid to get up close with a medium-sized tiger. I paid for Chelsea to get up close to a baby tiger. Once we got to the area and saw that the tigers were indeed alive and walking around, I was hesitant about letting Chelsea into the cage with a tiger by herself. I asked if she wanted me to go in with her. Deirdre said, "No Theresa, let her do it by herself." If something went wrong, I could hear my family say, "Why did you let her go in there by herself." That's when I told the attendant I would pay the extra money to go into the cage with Chelsea. The baby tigers were more like kids, not babies. There were two gentlemen there with us that interacted with the tigers. They also used my cell phone to take pictures and videos. I was so surprised that Chelsea didn't back down once she saw the tigers. She rubbed the tigers, played with their tails, and she even took a picture lying down with her head resting on the back of one of the tigers. Our fun with the exotic went on for at least 20 to 30 minutes. The time was only supposed to be 10-15 minutes, but it was early in the morning and the facility barely had customers. So, I'm sure that's why we were able to stay longer.

The medium sized tigers looked like grown horses. They did not interact with each other. They seemed to be a little in a daze. The business attested that they did not drug the tigers. However, I wasn't so sure but couldn't prove it. There were also two men in the larger cages with us. Unlike the baby tiger where we had to wash our hands and wear slip covers over our feet, we walked right into the large cage, which had some trees and small grass space. The area was shaded with peaks of the sun shining through. Again, we were able to take video and pictures of us lying down next to the large tigers. The time was not as long as because more customers started coming. This was a very exciting and fun moment. We could check, "Play with Tigers" off our bucket list. I don't really have a bucket list written out. I think I make it up as I live life. However, there are some things I would like to do before my soul leaves this earth. I would like to attend a Kentucky Derby and a high fashion runway show in New York during fashion week. There are a dozen more places I would like to travel as well. For now, I'm taking things one day at a time.

Those trips evoked thought and really brought to life an inner peace that I didn't know existed. Yes, I feel like I have captured what if feels like to have inner peace with yourself. I always felt that the biggest conflict is man versus self. For once in my life, I'm not having a battle within myself. I am sure that my life has purpose and meaning. I know that I was destined to be a mom, a sister, and an educator. I didn't say wife because I don't think I was good at being a wife and finding love or love finding me seems to be difficult these days.

Thailand provided me with the experience to make the best out of a bad situation. I thought myself, "Hey, you don't have your bags, but you do have a life. So, live it, girl!" So many times, people allow their situations and circumstances to stop them from doing what they were designed to do in life. From the time we are born, we are taught to listen to others and follow the dreams and goals that they have for us. We are never taught to just listen to our inner self, our inner being to hear what our spirit desires. We are so caught up in the rat race of life. We never take the time to smell the cheese to see if it is rotting. Living abroad afforded me the time to re-energize to replenish and examine who I am, who I want to be, and what I need to do to become what my heart and soul desires me to be.

CHAPTER 11

RETURNING HOME FOR THE FIRST TIME

Moving a thousand miles away from family and friends to the United Arab Emirates humbled us and strengthened our patience with people, but more importantly with one another. For the sake of gaining more patience, I did not give up, even when I could not understand the Arabic conversations that were held at school. Patience helped me not give up when I had to wait two months to be paid. I did not give up because I did not have a physical address. I did not give up when the water there broke off my daughter's hair and ruined all my underwear. The faucet water was very harsh on our clothes, skin, and hair. For the first time, I purchased a filter to put on the shower heads in our bathrooms. The filter contained vitamin C that help ed with the harshness of the water. I did not give up because I didn't know what to do with myself because I had more time on my hands. My point is never give up when you find that things are not what you are used to in life. Chelsea and I had to learn how to get through the tough times like missing Rylan's birthday. We had to learn how to make the most of going to work on Thanksgiving knowing our family and friends were in America enjoying a delicious Thanksgiving meal.

We went home for two weeks during our Christmas break. I was so excited and elated to see Rylan. He had grown so much in such little time. I could tell he had picked up some weight. His cheeks were so round and juicy looking. I wanted to just kiss on them. I held back my tears of joy in seeing him again. Returning to the UAE was harder than coming there the first time. I broke down at the airport and tightly hugged my son goodbye. I cried heavily. However, I tried not to let him see me cry. I knew that it would be several months before I got to kiss on those chubby cheeks and wrap my arms around him. Chelsea hugged me tightly and tears fell from her eyes. I wanted Rylan to come back with us so bad. I wished he could have experienced what we experienced even if it was just for a semester. I wanted him to experience visiting the tallest building in the world. I wanted him to experience riding the fastest rollercoaster in the world. It just didn't seem fair that he couldn't come back with us. I missed him so much.

After that, I video chatted with him every other day. I did the best I could to keep in touch and talk about what was going on in his world.

I hoped and prayed that he didn't resent Chelsea and me for going on this journey without him. We loved him dearly and wanted him to be with us.

CHAPTER 12

SPECIAL DAYS

Our first special day in the UAE was Chelsea's birthday. We had been in the UAE only eleven days and were still living in a hotel. We had no real transportation of our own, so we caught a taxis to get around Al Ain.

I wanted her birthday to be special. Chelsea was a social butterfly and had made friends with people in the hotel before I did. Everybody knew Chelsea. This was her eleventh birthday, and she was a thousand miles away from our family and friends. We had been in the country for eleven days and I only knew two other people who stayed at the same hotel, Deirdre and Tasha. However, I quickly made friends with a couple other young ladies, Tiffany and Meron, who later became my neighbors. Meron was the only one who had rented a car. She and Tiffany were sharing a rental car while we were staying in the hotel. As I said, I really wanted Chelsea's birthday to be special, but it was quite difficult since I didn't know where any of the grocery stores were nor did I have access to Walmart because there weren't any there. The way the government is set up, they will probably never have a Walmart. I didn't even have a car to get around. I didn't know where we were moving. I was on the hunt to find a place for us to live. I had told Chelsea that I would get her a cake and invite some of the other kids staying at the hotel to have cake with us. Well the entire day was spent running around to different rental properties and home stores, which prevented me from getting my baby girl a birthday cake. Inside I felt horrible and wanted to cry because this was the first year I hadn't bought my daughter a birthday cake or anything. She didn't seem upset. She played in the stores and helped pick out appliances and home décor. She was definitely a kid that didn't demand much if anything at all. I think she looked at the experience of moving and exploring a new country as a treat. She ended up playing cards with two little girls that were vacationing from Germany. She was content as she showed the girls how to play card games like Concentration and Speed.

The Fourth of July celebrations had nothing on National Day in the United Arab Emirates. I had never seen such love and celebration exhibited by a country. To be fair, I experienced a national day in the United States which was known as Independence Day. Here, the entire country was decorated in colors of red, black, green, and white. There were pictures of Sheik Zayed posted all over the city. You couldn't go anywhere without seeing someone showing their country patriotism for UAE. The cars had a picture of Sheik Zayed or the UAE flag all over it. The city had advertised all the different family fun activities that would be taking place in the different Emirates. Fireworks were shown in just about every Emirate. The country was turning 47 and all the locals as well as many of the Muslim expats that had made UAE their home for over a decade were super excited. I think the teachers were more excited to be off work for the first time since school started. Rightfully so, the school calendar was the worst I've ever seen. Also, the school system had changed the calendar in the middle of the school year. Teachers and staff members thought they would have two weeks off for spring break. However, the school system changed it to one week off for the teachers and staff and two weeks off for the students. If teachers had already booked trips during that time, then changes needed to be made. Also, the students and teachers were supposed to have three weeks off during Christmas or winter break. The school system, however, changed it to where teachers and staff would only have two weeks off and students had four weeks off. Another two weeks of the teachers' time was wasted on watered down professional development. As a matter of fact, some schools didn't even have professional development as the teachers slept during the day and socialized for two weeks.

Birthdays were special days to me. However, I became sad the weekend of Rylan's birthday. I was invited to two parties and didn't attend either one. All I could think about was how Rylan must feel on his seventh birthday and that his mother wasn't there. I was so emotionally hurt. I made sure I ordered him a special gift that would arrive before his birthday. Still, all I could think about was that *a gift doesn't take the place of mom*. I laid in bed weeping because I wasn't in the United States with my son celebrating his seventh birthday. I ordered pizza and drinks for his class at school and had them delivered on his special day.

Thanksgiving was another melancholy day. We had to work and go to school that morning. After work, Chelsea and I decided to go to the mall and have our own Thanksgiving dinner. We had dinner at TGIF. Chelsea ordered a cheeseburger and French fries and I ordered chicken salad. This was not a Thanksgiving dinner. We both were looking hurt in the face. Our eyes and lips drooped like two lost puppies. Our faces were void of any sign of happiness. We talked about what our family and friends were eating which made the situation worse. We ordered dessert just to cheer us up. I was teaching my daughter that food would help her sadness. That was definitely, not a good coping strategy, but we did feel a little better. We missed our family and the good southern food that delighted our soul. I feel like I had a slight win when Chelsea had the biggest smile on her face as a waitress placed the Whole Lotta Choc-Co-Lota Shake in front of her. That was the biggest shake I had ever seen in my life. It had a fudge brownie and donut attached to a stick hanging over the large glass with whip cream and chocolate syrup drizzled across the top. We both devoured that shake and walked out with full bellies and felt better emotionally, but we still missed home.

The kindergarten graduation and ceremony was a special day. The students hadn't been to school in two weeks; however, they all decided to show up for the graduation and ceremony. The graduation/ceremony was held a week before school was officially over for students. I did mention that the students stopped coming to school during Ramadan. None of the students came during the last week of Ramadan. This left teachers with plenty of free time to do absolutely nothing. There was some planning for next school year that took place, but more socializing than anything. The main hall of the school was decorated with pictures of the Sheiks, balloons, and graduation posters. Only mothers were in attendance. I had never seen a man attend any of the kindergarten ceremonies or parent meetings all year long. As a matter of fact, I don't believe the men were even invited. In a room of all women, some of the women still covered their entire face, exposing only their eyes. The kindergarten 2 students wore a black and gold graduation cap and a black and gold scarf that went over their heads. They did not wear a graduation gown, so you could see the girls' fancy dresses and the boys' bright white kanduras. As an Arabic song played over the loud speakers, the students walked in a line that was a little wobbly and disjointed. The mothers and aunts sat in adult black chairs on one side where they could see all the kindergarten 1 and kindergarten 2 students sitting in their miniature student chairs in a sloppy semi-circle. Between the chairs were two large blue rugs put together to make a "t." To the left of the carpet were awards and a table full of gifts wrapped in pastel wrapping paper. Behind the carpets were three huge pictures of three of the current sheiks.

The entire graduation was conducted in Arabic. I felt like a student attending school the same day they arrived in America and didn't speak or understand any English. However, I could figure out the special awards. Two students received awards for the best attendance during Ramadan, although they did not come to school the last week of Ramadan. I guess everything's relative – if the other kids didn't show up at all then the ones who showed up even a little become the "best" Other students received gifts and awards for their participation in volunteer work. Yes, our kindergarten students participated in community service projects. The chorus to "Pomp and Circumstance" played as students' names were called, and they walked over the blue rugs to collect their awards and gifts. Trying to take a group picture after each class was called was like trying to get six-month-old sextuplets to take a picture all smiling and looking the same way.

There were mothers and aunts I had never seen at the school before. Some of the mothers had dark brown skin and looked like an African-American which indicated that they were black Arabs. However, the son or the daughter was of a lighter skin. The mothers were very excited to take pictures of their kids receiving awards and gifts. Prior to the presentation of gifts, a couple of mothers started to go over to their child to take pictures of them in their graduation regalia. One of the staff members had to tell the mothers to wait to take pictures after the ceremony. After the ceremony, all the children went home with their mothers and the school was empty of students and full of socializing teachers. I was so thankful and relieved to have made it through first semester. Some expats didn't make it through first semester for various reasons. I felt accomplished and very proud of myself. My emotions of first semester were up and down. I wanted to leave and just go back home because I missed my son, because the country seemed to move so slow. However, I resisted the urge and continued to pray and talk with Chelsea about her experience.

Girl Talk

After being in Al Ain for a couple of weeks, Chelsea and I walked to the mall which was within walking distance from our townhome to walk around the mall. We noticed a school supply store inside the mall and wanted to get some books to read. School had not started for the fall and we wanted get prepared. There was a Muslim lady dressed in an Abaya with her three small children. The woman overheard Chelsea and me talking. She interrupted and asked, "Where are you from?"

"The U.S." we said in unison. We got asked that question a lot or, as I've noted, people assumed or people were from South Africa. The lady and I talked about the different educational resources for kids that we found in the store. The store was similar to Schoolbox which is a teacher store in the United States. However, some of the resources and materials were old and overpriced compared to U.S. prices for similar items. For example, some border paper cost about 90 AED ($24 USD). That same border paper in the United States would cost a lot less. Everything cost more in the UAE. I believe everything is imported. The woman's name was Dua and she was from Palestine. She had been living in the UAE with her children for the last two years because her husband worked at the university. Her English was fluent and lucid. However, she wanted me to work with her conversational English. I agreed to work with her until school started which was in a couple of weeks. So Dua and I met a couple of times at a coffee shop in the mall and once at her home.

Dua explained that prior to moving to the UAE, she lived in Saudi Arabia which was a lot stricter on women than the UAE. Women were not allowed to attend a movie theater or a sports function. She became very depressed living in Saudi Arabia. She had to cover her face whenever she was out. She could not go anywhere in public without her husband. She said that she felt very alone and became very depressed. She had no family and no friends in Saudi Arabia. She felt that moving to UAE saved her life. She liked that she had female friends whom she could communicate with and socialize with on a regular basis. She was a part of a women's book club. She worked as a journalist in Palestine and had received a few awards for her journalism work. She wrote stories that encouraged women and made them want to take care of themselves in a healthy way. However, she felt that she could not write as freely as she would like given certain laws about what women could or could not do whether in Saudi Arabia or the UAE. I definitely felt the same way. I believe women should have equal rights as men. Her two oldest children attended private school.

Sometimes the ladies at work would have girl talk. During one of the girl talks, I asked them what they thought about the United States. None of them had ever been to the United States. The first thing they all said was, "They have an open mind." They mentioned that their husbands studied in America and that their husbands told them that the men and women were very open-minded. Open-minded meant that the women and men were free to date whomever they wanted and could dress however they wanted. I noted that the women in the United States were very similar to them. For example, American women wanted a good life for their children and themselves. They mentioned that they learned about the U.S. from television and movies. I made sure that I told them "Things that you see on television and movies are not all real." When I asked the ladies what they did for fun, they just stared at me. One admitted "We mainly be with our kids." They explained the when they were younger and had a family of their own, they would meet up with their girlfriends to have tea. They all gave a look of *I wish I could have time to myself or hang out with friends*. These women are in their late 20s. One girl was 26 with four kids all under the age of seven. Another lady was 24 with four children as well. Another girl had three kids. Getting time alone was very difficult, even though they all had nannies caring for their children while they worked. Sometimes the nanny would watch their children while they did things at home like cook. For the most part, they said, "I like to raise my kids." There is a negative stigma that the women of UAE do not raise their children because they have nannies. The women I talked to were emphatic that they raise their children and they wanted to raise their children.

When I see children in the malls playing in the kids' play area, I noticed that most of the time they were with a nanny. If I could afford a nanny when my children were small and I worked full-time, I would have gotten a nanny. However, I think the families utilized nannies in the UAE because they were inexpensive and not because they were full-time working parents.

There are pockets of cliques of women in the UAE. The women who moved to the UAE at the same time tend to link up together. Some women link up based on nationality. For example, women from Egypt or Jordan tend to socialize together. Then the sorority women tend to socialize and hang out together. Women with children tended to hang together and the women without children did the same. The people that lived in the same apartment complex or neighborhood seemed to hang together. During my nightly runs, I noticed among a small group of women. Among them some wore an Abaya and some wore hijab and regular clothes. They were all walking and talking together. They all lived in the same neighborhood which is probably what brought them together, rather than their clothing.

I met one of my neighbors because Chelsea and her two daughters played together outside sometimes. One day I stopped to ask the mother if her oldest daughter could go to the mall. Her name is Shaima and she and her family were from Egypt. She was a semi heavyset lady. I realized that because as soon as she went into the house, she took off her Abaya and Shayla. She had on a fitted t-shirt and pants. The husband was an engineer and they had four kids, two boys and two girls. The family had lived in UAE for 10 years. They moved there right before the oldest was born. Shaima stated that she needed to ask her husband. She invited Chelsea and me into their villa, which turned out to be the same as mine, The floors were covered with different, large rugs. The television had what resembled the mecca and prayer on the screen. As we talked, Shaima spoke very little English so her two daughters did a lot of the translating.

She really missed living in Egypt. She loved Egypt and wanted to know what I knew about the country. I didn't know much about Egypt because I had never gone. A few friends had gone, but they never really said much about it other than that they saw some pyramids and it was quite dirty. But, I couldn't say that, so I said, "Not much." We talked about the quality of water in the UAE. Many people credited hair breakage and hair loss to the poor quality of the water. A friend had clumps of her hair falling out after she moved. Shaima confirmed that her hair had thinned out a lot since moving to the UAE. She really missed the men and women socializing together and partying. The men from western countries partied together in the UAE, but I had never heard or seen the Muslim men socialize or party together. The Muslim men and women were completely separated unless it was work related. It was the total opposite for the westerners. There were parties every week in Dubai and Abu Dhabi that were full of male and female expats. This was totally tolerated by the local law enforcement. It was a way for the country to get some of the money back from its expats.

Chelsea and I sat on the couch waiting for the little girl's dad to come down the stairs to give her permission to go to the mall with us. While we waited, Shaima went into the kitchen and came back with two glasses of lemonade and two slices of strawberry cake, served on a tray for Chelsea and me. She didn't ask if we wanted anything; she just brought out the cake and juice. That was customary in the UAE. Anywhere you visit from the post office to the hospital or a school, someone is there to serve you coffee, tea and dates. The cake was absolutely delicious. It melted in my mouth, taking away any reason to chew. The lemonade was a tad bit sweet. I thought, , "I hope this doesn't mess up my Weight Watchers points." I had just joined weight watchers the week before.

When the husband came down the stairs, he was very polite as well. I had seen him a couple of times in our neighborhood gym working out. He asked about my husband. I lied and said that he was working back in America with my son. I didn't want him to know that I was divorced because I didn't want him to view me as a bad person and someone his wife couldn't associate with. Shaima showed me her makeshift mint garden in the back yard, which appeared a little larger than ours. They definitely had more grass. Their dining room set was on their patio, though they also had patio furniture. This is where they had dinner every night. Both our patios were long but lacked width, so you could fit a dining set on one side and patio furniture on the other side. There were two sliding glass doors that led out from the living room and one that led out from the dining room. This was the beginning of a neighborly friendship.

To survive in any country, you must find friends that are similar to you in some way. The black community in the UAE is much different than the black community in the United States. For one, the black community in the UAE is small in size. Everyone knows everyone. Or they know someone that knows someone. The families with children stick together and the single people stick together. However, if someone needed help or support, everyone banded together and came to the rescue. There were times when I picked up other people's kids from school, and there were times when someone picked up Chelsea from school. All the black children that lived in Al Ain attended school online or attended the same private school, Manor Hall International School. There may be a few that attended other schools, but most attended Manor Hall.

There are different online Facebook groups or WhatsApp groups that are geared toward the various expat communities in UAE. There is a group for sororities and fraternities. There is a group for teachers, administrators, people moving in, people moving out, and people buying and selling things. The sense of community and family is present. When one child has a birthday, the community celebrates. When one family is in need, everyone helps. There is a sense of "We All We Got!" Does everybody get along all the time? No, that would be too perfect. As for me, I minded my business and didn't allow the problems of other people to become a part of my business.

I really enjoyed the girl time I spent at the family home of Jamila. Jamila was a teacher assistant for the special needs students at my school. She had such a kind heart and was always willing to help in any way. She was married to her first cousin and they had four kids. Out of the four, two were twin girls. She had invited Chelsea and me over to her father's house because her sister was preparing for her upcoming wedding. It was traditional for the women to get together and be pampered a week before the wedding.

When Chelsea and I arrived, we thought we had pulled up to a mansion. The house was huge. There were white lights that draped the front of the house. The lights indicated that a celebration was taking place. It was common for Emirati families to decorate their home during a celebration. There was a small house that looked like a pool house close to the carport. There were no garages there. Most people parked in a carport. The house was surrounded by a large brick wall. When we pulled into the driveway through the gate, little boys and girls were playing outside.

After parking the car, I asked one of the little kids who appeared to be about 6 years old, "Is Jamila here?" The kids ran inside to get Jamila.

We entered the house through large double doors to a large foyer with white marble floors. There were three other doors we could have entered. A little girl with almond skin and long black hair pointed to the door on the left and said Jamila was there. I later learned that she was Jamila's daughter. Jamila welcomed me with a big hug then introduced me to her family. Chelsea and I took our shoes off in the foyer upon entering the house. Jamila's family were all so kind, and some gave hugs and cheek-to-cheek kisses. None of the ladies were wore an Abaya or covered their face. They had long black hair that hung down to their waist. They all wore decorative print colored kanduras. All of them were in bare feet, including Chelsea and me. Jamila led us to another room, where we were given large plates of food. One was a rice and meat dish that had a spicy Indian flavor. The foods were very flavorful and different than what I was used to eating when it came to Emirati food. This food had an Indian flare to it. Jamila's older sister, whose mother was Indian had explained the food was indeed cooked with Indian spices. The food was prepared by the housemaids who, based on their physical features, appeared to be from India or an African country.

Jamila and her sister shared fathers. She was so open to sharing her family story. Earlier that year she lost her dad to cancer. He had four wives and sixteen children. His first and second wives only had one child by him. His third wife was Indian, and she had four kids by him. His last wife, which was Jamila's mom, had ten children by him. Her mother was Egyptian. Jamila laughed about how her dad liked women of different nationalities.

Jamila's older sister had a different mother and looked nothing like Jamila. Her mother was from India and was Jamila's father's third wife, whom I had the pleasure of meeting. She was an older Indian woman that showed her age by the deep creases in her hands and face. Her hair was covered, and she wore a colorful kandura that matched her Shayla. After eating the spicy dish that was Indian inspired,

After eating, Chelsea and I were led to another room off the foyer. The room was the size of a small New York City Apartment, maybe 400 square feet. The marble floor was covered with two huge Arabian print style rugs. They called this room the Majalis (room for entertainment). There was usually one for men and one for women. There were cushions placed together around the perimeter of the room to create a makeshift couch, leaving center of the room for dancing. The couch like cushions were supported with arm and back pillows. There were over 20 ladies and little girls sitting. Some were getting henna put on their hands, arms, and feet. Some were getting their eyebrows arched, and some were getting what appeared to be a facial.

There were four young girls from Ethiopia that were applying henna. They all wore a black abaya and Shayla. After asking me how far I wanted to get the henna up my arm, the girl instructed me to place my hands and arms inside of a white plastic bag. The bag was filled with a liquid that smelled like ammonia. I kept my arms in the bag for about 5 minutes. After drying my arms, she began using a mud-like clay to draw elaborate designs on my arms and hand. Another girl began to draw with the mud-like clay on my other arm. After they finished, I had to wait an hour before I could rub the clay off to display a beautiful design on my hands and arms. While getting the henna, I asked one of them about getting a facial. I wasn't sure that it was a facial because the paste was extremely white and applied with a small make-up brush. The entire face and neck were covered in this white paste. The only thing that was exposed was the eyebrows. I thought maybe they were exfoliating the skin. I definitely needed to exfoliate my skin. The sun there was doing a number on my skin. I asked the girl doing the henna about getting a facial by one of the Filipino women. "What is that?" I asked the girl. One girl looked at me strangely and asked her friend who was doing henna on my arm. She then looked at the Filipino woman and said something I couldn't comprehend. She then said in a low voice, "bleaching." "Oh, I like being dark, I don't want to bleach," I said. "It break out skin," the girl replied.

All the women were already very light-skinned. I didn't understand why they wanted to be even lighter. Those that had bleached their skin removed the pigmentation so much that their skin looked like a translucent glow, not lighter skin. Were Muslim women caught up in what the media had portrayed as beauty? The UAE seemed to be an intersection of many cultures, with different standards of beauty.

Later, Chelsea and I danced with Jamila and her sister. One sister even did a special dance that was dedicated to me as a guest. It was noted by another sister that the dance was for me when the sister danced and shook her long hair side to side in front of me. We had clapped and danced for hours until the sun went down.

I only saw one man the entire time I was there. One of Jamila's older brothers came into one of the rooms. Jamila introduced him to me. This was in the room adjacent to the henna room. I spoke and wondered if I should extend my hand for a handshake. I decided against it and just spoke. I didn't know if it would have been appropriate. In Muslim culture, men should not shake the hand of a woman unless she extended her hand first.

I didn't see any of the men that lived in the house because the men had a separate side of the house where they entertained. They also had a different entrance to the house. I enjoyed talking to the sisters about their culture and traditions. The oldest sister, whose mother was Indian, spoke three languages and had a master's degree in technology. She was very proud that her mother was one of the only wives to have a college education.

The large family of sisters and children dined at the father's house weekly. The women only showed their hair and cheek kissed their brothers. The only men the women socialized with was their brother. The ladies were not allowed to show their hair or cheek kiss their male cousins with whom they did not interact. The girls and boys in the family are separated at the age of 10.

The women didn't know anything other than what they had been exposed to by their culture. They never played a board game with their male cousins. They never really had healthy debates with any males. They had been separated from socializing with men outside of their family all their lives. It did not bother them that they did not interact with other men or to hear the opinions of other men outside of their family and government leaders. They took their direction from the Quran which told them that men should be over them. I don't agree with this and I think men take advantage of this concept to benefit themselves.

One of my staff members expressed that she was more of a take-charge-kind of woman. That reminded me of most of the American women I knew. She had a bachelor's and master's degree in business administration. She wanted to earn her Ph.D, but her husband did not want her to do get it. So, she suggested that he earn a Ph.D. Needless to say, neither one of them is working on a PhD. She felt that her husband would feel uncomfortable with her earning a higher degree than he. He wanted to be control everything including her. I wanted to take a picture with her without her face covered to keep on my phone and she said that she had to ask her husband. He responded, "No, never." As a result, she did not take the picture with me.

She shared issues about her marriage that mirrored the same issues of my married friends in America. That is, it seemed like there was a universal problem with men. The women want more romance, and the men lacked the ability to be more romantic. That is not to say all men are not romantic or that all women want to be romanced. She talked about how her husband did not like how she spoke to him in a demanding manner. For example, a simple request such as "Close the door" was like she was giving him orders and he did not like that. Wow! That sounded like my former marriage. My ex-husband felt like I was giving him orders when I made requests. She said that she had to pray about it and read the Quran for guidance. The solution for her was to use a gentler voice and make her request in a more loving way. Once she did that, she saw a difference in her husband. She said he would speak in a more loving tone with her and be more affectionate with her. I definitely can see how this would work for her and other situations. It's not what you say, but how you say it.

Traditions

There are many traditions that exist in every culture. In Bali, they don't allow a babies' feet to touch the ground for a year. In the United Arab Emirates, they cut the babies' hair at two months old. Traditions are what makes us a group of people unique. On this journey I learned to embrace the uniqueness that exist amongst people, cultures, race, and nationalities. Chelsea and I have become more and more closer to God and His purpose of our life. Each day we read a devotional, analyze a scripture, and give God praise by playing a gospel song. Chelsea learned about the different kinds of peace. This journey has brought about a peace that is only given from God through Jesus. We have the kind of peace that exudes respect for God's will and we are ok with our situation regardless of the circumstances now or future circumstances.

The Brown girls have created our own tradition as a mother daughter duo. Daily, we prayed, we listened, and we praised God. It brings tears to my eyes when I think about how Chelsea is gaining knowledge about the world, but more importantly a relationship with God. She is no longer on medication for ADHD and she is thriving and doing well. She understands that her help and opportunities come from God. Proverbs 4:23 "Carefully guard your thoughts because they are the source of true life." We are responsible for our thoughts whether they are good or evil. Your thoughts will dictate your feelings which will transpire into your actions. We must learn to keep our thoughts on positive, healthy, and meaningful.

There are a couple Christian churches in Al Ain. Church is held on Fridays. Friday was considered to be the Holy day here. I attended a Christian church very close to my house. They had praise and worship like any normal church. The choir was predominately of African descent. The music was so soulful and hyped up. They were live and energetic. The preaching was conducted by a Caucasian male. He used

PowerPoint to help deliver the message. However, I got a little lost trying to look at the busy PowerPoint and listen to the message. Although I believe the message was about telling other people about the goodness of God and inviting them to come to church.

There is also a catholic church near my villa. They have service on Thursday evenings. I've only gone to a catholic church a few times in my life. Those were times when I attended Eastside Vicariate in Detroit, Michigan. I was raised traditionally of Christian faith. I've never been taught other religions or their beliefs. As an adult, I've learned about other religions through study and now through my experience living in a Muslim country.

One day at work, I was walking down the hall and I noticed the head cleaning staff member from Sri Lanka. She was carrying a white plastic grocery bag with pictures in it. I looked at the big and squinted my eyes. It appeared to be a picture of the white version of Jesus. She must've noticed my squinting eyes and look of confusion because she slowly pulled part of it out of the bag that confirmed my vision. She said in a soft voice as if she was telling a secret, "Madam, I laminate for the home." I then asked, "Are you a Christian?" She replied, "Yes." I then gave a warm smile and said, "Ok. Me too." That was our "Me too" moment in this predominately Muslim work environment. She smiled back and then continued to walk.

Chelsea and I have engaged in the power of setting a tradition and vision. It's not enough to just engaged in traditions without having a vision of what we desired. We desired to be a part of God's purpose and living in His will. We wanted to be conscious and aware of what we do every day was and still is aligned with God's purpose for us. We set the tradition of praying and analyzing the word of God. We took time to truly think about how it related to our lives. It was hard to imagine that God could bless us beyond our own imagination because it just hadn't happened. However, we were willing to put it to the test. So, Chelsea and I prayed and asked God to bless us with some of our wildest dreams.

Ramadan

The first time I heard of Ramadan was when I lived in New Jersey with my dad. I only knew that it was for Muslims. Ramadan is a time of year which Muslims all around the world fast or give up food and drinks during daylight hours. When they break the fast in the evenings, it is called Iftar. Mosques and other organizations set up tents around the city to feed people during Iftar. During this time, I heard and received WhatsApp messages that said, "Ramadan Kareem" and "Ramadan Mubarak." They have two different meanings, Ramadan Kareem means have a blessed Ramadan and Ramadan Mubarak means Happy Ramadan. During this time, the entire country adjusted the work hours. My students attended school from 8:30 to 12:00, and Chelsea attended school from 9:00 to 1:00 pm. The malls, doctors' offices, and stores had different hours. As of this writing, I made a dentist appointment for 10:30 pm. The city is completely empty and barren of cars on the road during Ramadan during certain hours of the day. The mall and many stores were closed between 3:00pm and 8:00pm. They reopened at from 8pm to 2am. My work hours have changed as well. Before the fast, e worked from 7:45am to 1:45pm. During the fast, I worked from 8:00am to 1:00pm. At Chelsea's school there is a special room for students that are fasting and one for students that are not fasting.

The exact day of Ramadan is not established until the first moon of the ninth month of the Islamic calendar. During Ramadan you are not allowed to eat or drink in public. Chelsea and I kept looking outside to determine the phase of the moon to see if Ramadan would begin the next day. It felt like Americans looking to see if the groundhog would see his shadow to determine if spring would come early.

The entire country was excited about Ramadan. There were commercials on the television and radio advertising different Ramadan sales. It almost felt like Christmas in America. However, it's almost as if night and day swapped places. During the daylight hours the city was like a ghost town, and at night the streets and stores were packed full of people. On the radio people were asked about what Ramadan meant to them. One young girl mentioned that Ramadan was about her spending time with her family and friends. Another young man mentioned that it was a spiritual time to be thankful. I chose to participate in Ramadan and only partake in water and tea during daylight hours. I wanted to know what everyone else was experiencing. By 1:00pm, I had a headache, and my stomach was hurting. However, I said a prayer and kept going on with my day. I noticed that when it was time for me to break my fast, I couldn't eat as much as I normally would if I weren't fasting. If I tried to eat normal as if I wasn't fasting, I became nausea. One of the Emirati teachers shared that when I break the fast that I should eat a little at a time. "Try eating some dates Ms. Theresa," I was told.

The only Muslims that are excluded from fasting are small children, people that are ill, pregnant women, and women that are on their menstrual cycle. Did you know that women that are on their menstrual cycle are not allowed to enter the Mosque? They are considered to be unclean. The ladies at work said that if a woman dies while she is on her menstrual cycle, she is automatically accepted into Paradise. Paradise is used simultaneously like Heaven. Some of Chelsea's classmates suggested she fast. Before Ramadan began, she said in a matter of fact tone, "I'm going too fast." She changed her mind once the Ramadan began. She took her lunch to school, which a room was provided for students that were not fasting.

There are a lot of things a person should be aware of during Ramadan. I quickly learned that you are not allowed to drink anything in public when a man raised his fist and begin to shake it at my friend for drinking water in her car. You can't even chew gum or eat in public during Ramadan. One girl confessed to getting a ticket when another driver reported her license plate to the police for drinking in her car in public. The result is a hefty fine and could lead to jail time. I didn't see the police use force and anytime I had an encounter with them, they were very kind to me.

During this time, I'd been able to be read my bible more. The first Scripture I read during my fast was Mathew 4:4: *Man shall not live on bread alone, but on every word that comes from the mouth of God.(New International Version).* There were so many times my stomach felt pain and discomfort, I wanted to just say, *That's enough. God knows my heart.* But there was something about the ladies at work that made me really want to stick with it. I wanted God to see my sacrifice and anoint me in a special way. I wanted to experience the power of manifesting things in my life. I wanted to breathe healing life into friends that were sick or having an emotional break down in life. I had to keep fasting, praying, and reading the Word. If you want something different in life, you must do something different in life.

The Ramadan schedule had Chelsea and me home from school and work by 2:00pm each day. We talked about all kinds of things. She talked about living in New Zealand and the number of Americans that live in New Zealand. We had mother-daughter conversations about puberty that started when she asked while pointing between her legs, "Mom do you shave the hair down there?" I responded, "Some women shave or wax their pubic hair." "Why do they do that?" she inquired. I explained that women wax or shave their hair for sanitary reasons. She was quite surprised, but I could tell she was taking it all in. She laughed that she would have hair everywhere and wouldn't do neither. We both laughed at how musty she would be smelling and people running away from her.

During Ramadan, I meditated and reflected on Scriptures that supported my fast and that would bring more understanding to my journey. I was missing Rylan more and more as the days creeped by. He was finally out of school for the summer and still could not be with his mother. The plan was for him to come with my girlfriend, and then he, Chelsea and I would fly back to the states once we got out of school. But, my ex-husband backed out of the deal. So, I decided to send Chelsea back to the states a week for her last day of school. I still had another three weeks before my last day of school. Also, she wanted to be home for the Fourth of July festivities.

I understood her homesick feeling. I was feeling the same way. We had not been home in six months. We were getting quite agitated and constantly seeing women in Abayas and men wearing Kanduras made it worse. It was a reminder that we were nowhere near American soil. I knew I needed to pray more when I imagined myself snatching the black sheer fabric off the face of the Muslim women, "What are you doing?" Some women struggled with one hand holding it up to their face as they walked around the mall. Other women used a special face garment that went around their head and covered their face except their eyes. This is not done in all Muslim cultures, but highly used in the Emirati culture. When I asked about why women conceal their face from the public, I was given several reasons. For instance they did it out of tradition, because their husband requested it, and to prevent other men from seeing them.

We were two weeks into Ramadan and my stomach was getting used to basically eating one meal a day. I could have eaten more than one meal, but I refused to wake up early or in the middle of the night to eat. We incorporated daily devotion into our afternoons. That's when I learned that my baby girl was lacking knowledge of basic bible teachings. Chelsea knew the Lord's prayer but didn't know who Adam and Eve were. She went to a Christian daycare until she was five years old and attended children's church when I took her to church. So, I was surprised when she did not know who Adam and Eve were.

We used different Bible plans on the Bible app to have our daily devotion. We even incorporated Christian songs, so we did praise and worship. The holy month of Ramadan reminded me so much of fasting and praying at my home church. I knew that things would be changed in a mighty way during my fast.. However, I was expecting things would go from one extreme to another. I was feeling at peace. I mean I really felt an assurance and confidence that God was working in my life in a mighty way. That kind of peace that I felt was one that could only come from God.

One afternoon during Ramadan, I opened my email to find some news that changed everything. I saw the email was from personnel.

Greetings,

We are pleased to extend our appreciation to you for all your efforts and contributions with ADEK. We would like to inform you that your employment contract will be terminated effective from August 25, 2018 inclusive of the notice period. You will be notified of the date of commencement of the necessary exit procedures.

Best Regards,

Personnel Services Division

Just like that I was being told that I would no longer have a position when school restarted after the summer. I needed to pray more now than ever before. My emotions went from "God is in control" to "Fuck this country." I wasn't the only one being released. The school system was getting rid of the Academic Vice Principal position and all the expats that served in a leadership capacity. There were hundreds of expats that were just like me now looking for employment. This country had the power to let people go at any given time. I watched a video where a man spoke about his friend working in Dubai and showed up to work with her things already boxed up and was told that she no longer had a job.

There were a couple of teachers that were terminated in the middle of the school year and had 30 days to leave the country. Imagine packing up your entire family to relocate out of the country, spending thousands of dollars packing up your old home, paying moving expenses ,storage facilities, and trying to make your new residence feel like home to only be told after one year, your services were no longer needed. I didn't know what to think. My emotions were on a rollercoaster. This meant that I was required to leave the country at the end of the school year. My faith in God that He would see me through this was unwavering. I continued to fast and praise Him and applied for jobs at the same time. Faith without works is dead.

The school system stated that they would keep the last two checks until one completed the exit process. The process involved moving completely out of your apartment or villa and getting a clearance letter from the management company to say you did not cause any damages. Next, I needed to have the power and cable turned off and to pay the final bill to get a clearance letter from them that I would take the school system. So where was I supposed to stay while I was doing all of this? In a hotel that the school system would not pay for. Luckily, I had friends that were still staying with whom we could stay for a few weeks. Completing those tasks did not include the process of selling my furniture and household items. Once all those things were complete and I had clearance letters from each institution I needed to submit, I had to wait an additional 10 business days before they would deposit my End-of-Service check into my local account in the UAE. I refused to leave this country without my money. The way they conducted business let me know I better not get on a plane without my money because I would never see it! The month in which I would exit was considered to a holy month, but there was nothing holy about losing my job.

As Ramadan continued, the students' attendance decreased tremendously. Some schools had zero students attend school. Most of the Muslim teachers slept at school when there were no children. If a few students came to school, they would combine the classes and teachers would take turns reading the Quran and sleeping. This was the biggest waste of time I'd ever heard of on the school level. The teachers would be tired from staying up all night socializing with family, eating, and praying. The ladies at work said that they were not allowed to have sex during the day with their husbands during Ramadan. They could not participate in any activities during the day other than work and pray. This was reflected at night when the stores and streets became extremely crowded. Chelsea and I decided to get ice cream at nearly one o'clock in the morning and the streets were filled with cars and people walking and conducting business you would ordinarily see during the day.

The school and government agencies were closed for the end of Ramadan. The end of Ramadan is called Eid. I ended my fast one week earlier. I probably could have continued, but my heart was no longer in it. Apparently, hearts of some of the Muslims weren't in it either. There was a line of local Muslims in the drive thru at McDonalds at 2 o'clock in the afternoon. I did not believe this breach of Ramadan rules and regulations, so my friend took pictures to prove it. Various cities celebrated the end of Ramadan by having firework shows, parties, and lots of store discounts. The malls were completely packed with local and expat Muslims. I had never seen the mall so crowded with people.

That same weekend a viral message on WhatsApp was circulating among the expat administrator groups. The email message was stating that administrators that were non-renewed or their contract was being terminated should call the hotline for the Ministry of Education to be considered for one of the new positions. Some felt that this was a lifeline, I felt like it was my way to go home without being a quitter or known as a runner. A couple of my friends suggested that I call the number just in case. However, I refused to call, and my spirit would not allow me to call. I was adamant that if they didn't want me, I didn't want them. This reminded me of the many times my mother would say, "Never stay where you are not welcomed." At that point, the company had not sent out an official email stating they would provide us with an opportunity for new jobs, and I was not going to beg for one. The God that I serve will never forsake me, nor will He have me begging for a job, food, friends, man, or any other material things.

People tend to devalue themselves on the job and in relationships. People will treat you how they see you treat yourself. I am a valuable educator and motivator. I understand and know what I bring to the table which is why I don't mind eating alone. We must learn to trust God no matter the circumstances. We must lean on our faith and not doubt God's plan for our life.

During this time, I was even more excited about my journey and life than ever before. I knew that I controlled my destiny and how I had possessed the power of Jesus within me. We must learn to trust the process of seeking our purpose and aligning it with God's purpose. My dreams were becoming more and more vivid. I was dreaming more often and could remember my dreams a lot clearer. One of my dreams consisted of me being inside an empty money booth with only a few dollars flying around me. Then it switched to me being surrounded by a lot of money. I was like a kid playing in a ball pit, but instead of it being balls, it was money.

I am not a dream interpreter, nor do I know one, so I Googled what the dream meant. I read that when a person dreams of gaining money or have a large store of it in a dream it is an indication that you feel capable of achieving whatever goal or objective that you have in life. One article stated that dreams of receiving money typically leave the dreamer content and satisfied with their life and current decisions. Those interpretations were exactly how I felt and even more. I was thankful to God for Ramadan and the Muslim women that read the Quran around me. It motivated me to gain a better relationship with God. I implement the power he has given me, the power to manifest things in our life is a gift from God that I am just now understanding and using. Ramadan was an interesting experience and one that I will never forget, and I still have much respect for the Muslim religion.

It took me moving to a Muslim country to understand and experience God's power and purpose in my life.

CHAPTER 13

BLACK IN THE MIDDLE EAST

There are so many times when I am present in the room but feel like I don't exist. This is because a language is spoken that I don't understand. At work many conversations have taken place by staff members that will go from speaking with great force to speaking softly. In my head I'm thinking, "What the hell am I doing here again?" "Who are they talking about?" "Did they know that teacher was really that bad?" I retreated to my head anytime the conversations would take off for a long stint. Every now and then, my principal would say, "Tell Ms. Theresa in English." That came out perfectly in English. She spoke some English but felt more comfortable speaking Arabic. I remember a time when she was upset with me about not verifying a duty schedule and she had signed off on the paper. The duty schedule had a name of teacher that was no longer at the school. She yelled at the Head of Faculty because she didn't know enough English to yell at me. I felt bad for the Head of Faculty.

Many times, people will ask, "How do you feel being black in an Arab country?" I always thought that was a funny question. I'm black wherever I go. I don't see myself as being different. I am comfortable being black. I've been black all my life. I don't know how to be another race. I can't identify with another race. I don't think I am treated differently because I am black. When living in the United States, there are thoughts that cross your mind like, "Did she say that because I am black?" "Are they following me around the store because I am black?" Race is a factor in the United States whether people want to believe it or not. However, I don't see race as an issue living in the middle east. However, I think that people abroad have been brainwashed to think that the lighter the skin, the more beautiful the person. I was shocked when another administrator shared a story with me that took place at her school.

She was going home to the United States for a week to attend a wedding and her mother was having surgery. The Muslim ladies at her job asked her to bring them back a blonde hair blue eyed white man. It was said in a joking manner, but there was some truth to their joke. My friend is a brown skinned black girl. So, she asked, "You don't want me to bring back dark man?" The women said, "No dark man, no brown man. We want white man." These Muslim women were not interested in a man of color or even a dark-skinned Caucasian. They wanted a white man with blonde hair and blue eyes. My friend even shared how some of the staff members discussed the different bleaching creams. Even in other countries we visited such as Thailand, there were bleaching cream billboards advertising the latest bleaching creams. I was completely baffled by the advertisement and even the desire for people that are much lighter than myself or would be viewed as Caucasian in America want to be even lighter. We must move past the dynamics of race and color. When visiting India, I saw people that were even darker skin than I was, and race issues seemed like it was nonexistent. The issues and challenges that many of the people face in the middle east and Asia are related to nationalism and classism, not race.

I never discussed race or the object of skin color with Chelsea because I don't want her to see it as a factor. I want her to be the best person that she can be regardless of her race or in spite of her skin color. I saw a post on Facebook from a girl that was displeased about one of the black male stars from Black Panther hugged up with a Caucasian girl. She expressed her anger about black men dating white women or women that were very light-skinned. People were commenting about how the girl was insecure and she was jealous and had other issues. I didn't agree with the comments. They were passing judgement on a young lady they didn't know. However, the way she expressed her anger toward black men dating white women or very light-skinned women was the wrong way. I feel like I knew exactly where she was coming from. As a dark-skinned black woman that is constantly shown images of black men with women that are light-skinned or white causes you to question if your skin color is good enough for the black male. Living in the middle east, I've seen black men with women that were white and other races and thought, "Even overseas the black women can't catch a break."

I haven't experienced racism living in the middle east, but I have heard that it does exist. A black friend of mine that was teaching in Abu Dhabi shared a story of a student being picked on because she was darker than the other students. The student was a black Muslim. After the students were taken to the school social worker and the parents got involved, the next day the student that was the aggressor told my friend, "My parents said I can't touch you because your skin is dirty." Also, another friend shared that the students were caught teasing another student because he was also a black Muslim. She noted that the Muslims didn't want to acknowledge that African slaves were used which is one-way black Muslims came about.

One of my administrator friends had a really hard time at her school. I'll name her Karen. The stories she would share of the racism that took place in her school was quite astounding. Her principal who I met twice looked like a brown-skinned black person. If you took off her Abaya and placed her in America she would be seen as African American. Her principal did not like being brown skinned. She talked about the different bleaching creams she purchased to obtain the bright skin. However, she still struggled with her cuticles, elbows, and knees. She even made a comment, "No, dark not good." It was like she was oblivious that my friend was black or that her family was of African descent.

Once a black Arab substitute came to the school to sub for a teacher that was absent. The principal immediately told my friend, "Watch that subs. Someone needs to stay in her room." However, any time other substitutes would come to the school she would say nothing. In fact, she would engage in conversations with them and offer them tea and dates. That was the same school that the parents expressed concern about an Egyptian teacher teaching their children and the Egyptian teacher was transferred. Stories like that are rare, but they do exist.

There were ways that Chelsea and I tried to adjust to make this country like our home. One of the ways was through the use of Set Television. SetTv allowed us to watch American television shows through Amazon Fire Stick. Chelsea and I were watching television and a Chick fila commercial came on. We both looked at each other and our eyes instantly became teary. We both let out an angry moan that said we wished we were home. Watching CNN gave me a sense that I was home and I knew what was going on. I listened to all the Trump antics that made me embarrassed to be an American abroad. It was hard to believe that he would call American citizens, "sons of bitches" and think that it was ok. We tried to adapt to the country as much as we could without losing our identity or what we stood for. So, being silly in the mall and dancing in stores helped us to just be ourselves.

I felt like the Muslim women in UAE were living under a smoke screen and it was hard for them to just break free and be themselves. I felt free in expressing myself which caused some issues at work. One day at work I was in the office laughing with two other ladies. The laughing got a little loud where my principal could hear her in her office a few feet away. She called into the office to ask who was in the office and to say that we were laughing too loud. Also, she wanted us to know that a man was in the building. She then asked the staff member to tell me to come to her office. When I entered the office, she asked me to take a seat in one of the chairs posted in front of her desk.

Her office was nicely decorated. Upon entering her office, she had two large size leather couches on each side of the room with a nice wooden rectangular coffee table in the center. The table had an old basket huge basket of assorted chocolates that were given as a gift for International Women's

Day from the school district a few months ago. I didn't understand why she didn't give most them away to the staff. I thought maybe she was being a little stingy at the time. Now the chocolates were starting to stale sitting on the coffee table.

She asked in English as best she could in her Arabic accent, "Theresa is it ok to have noise in the school in America?" I was so dumbfounded by the question that I had to look puzzle as if I didn't understand the question. So, she asked again, but in a different way, "Do you make noise at school in America?" I literally started to laugh, but I held it together and said, "Yes, in America we laugh and make noises." She looks at me in a shameful manner and says, "In the school you should not make loud noise. A man is in the building." The fact that a man's presence made it inappropriate to make loud noise. I found that to be just plain silly.

"Ok, I understand" as I always did. However, I wanted to say, "This is some bullshit!"

The women are taught to be shy and silent. They are taught to be silent and have no voice or speak up for injustices. In fact, it is against the law in the UAE to have a public protest. Many of the administrators were upset about the abolishment of their positions and wanted to write a letter however, many disagreed to the possible ramifications of the government. As I reflected on my freedom as a woman born in America, I appreciated my voice and my rights to express myself.

Middle East Transitions

Bank Debacle

When we first arrived in UAE we were only given one banking option with one bank. This was the bank that our payroll deposits would go into. We set up accounts during the first week we were in Abu Dhabi. We had no idea about any other banks and we couldn't set up an account with any other banks because we didn't have our work visa or passport. My passport was being used to process my visa and Emirates ID. The bank offered us a credit card on the spot during orientation, but it would take another month or so to receive it. Even though we signed for paperwork at the time to obtain an account with the only preferred bank we still had to contact the bank again once we received our Emirates ID and Visa inside our passport. Talk about home service. The bank associates would come to your home to pick up documents and have you sign off on the additional paperwork. One month later I received three credit cards in the mail. I had no idea that I was getting that many credit cards. One had a limit of thirty thousand dirhams, and two for twenty thousand dirhams. That was equivalent to about nineteen thousand USD worth of credit. In addition to the credit cards, a bank associate called me once a week offering me loans. I opted not to take out a loan however, it was very tempting. I was thinking about taking out a loan and pay off my credit cards in the United States, so my credit score can improve. However, I opted to just slowly pay them off myself. However, many expats have gotten caught up in taking out loans. Some have taken out loans and try to skip town and get caught at the airport.

Meanwhile, I used one of the credit cards, while I was waiting on my payroll salary that took two months to receive. I should've paid it off right away, but I didn't. When I finally sat my butt down and looked at the interest rate, I almost had a heart attack. The interest rate was a lot higher than what I was paying on my credit cards in the United States. I overpaid one of the credit cards and asked the bank to transfer the overpayment into my regular account. They stated that they would not be able to do that and that I had to call back after the credit card was closed which would take a couple of weeks. Dealing with National Bank of Abu Dhabi was like pulling wisdom teeth and scratching on a chalkboard at the same time.

Another issue I had with the bank dealt with international wire transfer. I transferred several thousand dollars into my U.S. account however, the bank couldn't tell me where the money was and why it was taking so long to transfer. It took two weeks for the money to transfer into my U.S. account. That was the first and last time I used that bank to do an international wire transfer. From that point, I withdrew my money and went to a money exchange center to wire money into my U.S. account. It is there the next day. I eventually opened an account with another bank and had my payroll check deposited into that account. During orientation in Abu Dhabi, we only had one choice of banking.

It takes a minimum of 45 days before the bank will officially close your account and issue you a bank clearance letter. That is needed when you have decided to end your work contract and receive your bonus pay. You receive one month's salary for each year you work your contract. So, your bonus pay adds up. If someone would like to payroll to deposit your paycheck into another bank, you must receive a letter from your current bank that states you don't have an outstanding balance on credit cards or loans. Many expats have complained to each other about having a hard time getting letters from banks. However, they dare not complain to the government.

CHAPTER 14

WELCOME TO DUBAI

Chelsea and I made our first visit to Dubai for a weekend visit. Dubai is about one hour and fifteen minutes from Al Ain. We stayed at a nice hotel that wasn't far from the Dubai Mall and Burj Khalifa. Burj Khalifa is the world's tallest building. We decided to go on a Desert Safari on the first day and then visit Burj Khalifa on the second day. When driving into Dubai, the skyline looks almost unreal. The buildings look like miniature toys from a distance. The scenery just doesn't look real! It reminds me of a kid playing with a mini city toy. It's quite amazing to clearly see the details and unique designs of each building. Chelsea and I looked in awe. She began taking pictures of the buildings from inside the car. I tried to slow down on the highway, so she could get a better glimpse, but one of the hitchhikers thought I was slowing down for him, so I sped back up and continued down the highway.

Dubai is very different from Al Ain and Abu Dhabi. I found Dubai to be more non-traditional. We didn't see a lot of Muslim women wearing Abayas and the men wearing Kanduras. There were a lot plainer clothes wearing Muslims. I was told that when Muslims visit other countries they will not wear an Abaya or Kandura. However, the women would still cover their hair. The ladies at work would show me pictures of themselves vacationing and not wearing an Abaya. They showed their pictures as if they were trying to prove something to me. One coworker showed me a picture at her sister's wedding party. After the wedding, the next day the bride has a party and all the ladies dress in gold. She looked stunning. She had on a Mr. Tee like gold neck piece that draped down pass her chest and several gold bracelets. She wore bold make-up with foundation that looked two shades lighter than her skin. It was not uncommon for the women to have on foundation that was two to three shades lighter than their natural skin color. I wondered if it was because there was no brand that matched their skin tone or if they just wanted to look lighter. I was starting to think it was the later.

I attended several parties in Dubai and they all seemed to be a lot different than any of the other parties I had attended in Al Ain and Abu Dhabi. Parties were advertised on the radio, flyers, and by word of mouth. Once you attended a day party, you could expect to get some time of email advertising the next day party. Dubai seems to have more of a variety of professionals from all over the world. The people in Dubai seemed to be more fast paced and worldly. I rarely saw the traditional nose kisses the men gave each other when greeting each other. I rarely saw the men holding hands or linked up by their pinkies walking down the street like I did in Al Ain. Dubai was much more relaxed. You could walk down the street or in the mall wearing shorts or a skirt and sleeveless tops without all the stares.

Dubai reminded me of New York City in which there were lots of people from different parts of the world. Most of the people that lived in Dubai were professionals that earned a generous salary. However, I did come across a few military professionals that were docked in Dubai for whatever reason. It was very easy to meet these people at the different parties or brunches. The brunches were very popular and somewhat expensive in Dubai. The most popular brunch was the Saffron Bruch at the Atlantis Hotel. That was best one I've attended. There was a live DJ, dancers, all you can eat buffet of all kinds of food, and all types of alcohol you can possibly think of.

People that I've met in Dubai say that the cost of living is too expensive, so they opt to live outside of Dubai in one of the neighboring cities or Emirates and commute into work. Dubai has a lot of luxury and convenience to offer which usually means, there are a lot of low class workers nearby. They definitely do not live in Dubai. One day as I was being driven to the airport, the driver showed me some of the housing of some of the low paid workers. It looked like long rectangular rows of brick boxes. It was very similar to where the girl who cleaned my villa lived. She lived in a community that was full of rectangular brick housing lined up next to each other. You could see where some of the people hung their clothes outside to dry. It was hard to imagine that Dubai was known as one of the richest countries in the world, but people were living in small square studio brick made homes. The housing accommodations were usually paid for by the company that brought them from their countries to work or a portion of the rent was taken out of their payroll check.

A lot of the lower paid workers do not add to the economy in Dubai. Most of the money is put back into the economy by the professionals. The lower paid workers do not spend money of fast food restaurants, clothes, car rentals, and high-priced groceries. They save and send a lot of their money home when and if they get paid. Yes, I was told by a couple of the low paid workers that sometimes the company would not pay them. One African girl from Nigeria was hired and brought to UAE to braid hair. She told me that the girl that brought her from Nigeria hadn't paid her in two months. She was taking clients on her days off to make money to send home to her family. Another girl that worked for one of the private schools as a cleaner stated that the school hadn't paid some of them in a month. There was nothing they could do about it and they were too afraid to do anything about it. They didn't want to be sent home and miss out on any money that was due to them.

The way payroll was handled in the UAE was like nothing I had ever experienced. The teachers would get paid on one day and the administration would get paid a couple days later. Then, a couple of days before anyone was supposed to be paid an email was sent that explained that everyone would get paid on the same day later than what was expected. This was a process went into effect immediately. Which was the day before people were expecting to get paid. They were the government, so they could do whatever they wanted and there was nothing you could do about it but call any of your creditors and changed the date for when they would take money out of your account. The government basically ran the show in Dubai and all other Emirates.

Dubai had a lot of tourist attractions that Chelsea and I would engage in from time to time. Everything was quite pricey, so we were limited in what we did. However, we did take advantage of the flash sales. We went to the Aquaventure Waterpark and Dolphin Encounter for half price at the Atlantis. That was the best waterpark we had ever gone to.

Chelsea loved the 1km lazy river pool. There were so many different types of water slides. The scariest for me was the Poseidon's Revenge. Chelsea shocked me when she took a leap of faith and went down the slide, Leap of Faith. The dolphin encounter was an awesome experience.

We were put in groups of 5-6 people to interact with dolphins alongside two dolphin trainers. We learned interesting facts about the dolphins such as they could hold their breath for no more than 10 minutes. Also, they shed their skin every two hours. We got a chance to stroke the back of the dolphin, dance with him, and hug him. There was a photo nearby to capture all the moments. Afterwards we were able to see the pictures and buy what we liked. The pictures were overpriced, but that was expected.

Self-Reflection

I couldn't believe that they'd canceled my contract after only one year, I was in the same situation that I'd been in back in the U.S. I asked myself, "What are you doing girl?"

"What do you want out of life?"

"What are you putting out into the universe that exudes career change?" I couldn't come up with an answer that said I wanted more change in my life. I had packed up everything, gave my dog away and uprooted my daughter for one year of living abroad. "I signed up for three years, not one year" I thought. I had become accustomed to enjoying silence and living a low-key life. I enjoyed working in a culture that I didn't have to be a part of because I didn't speak the language. I wasn't ready to leave UAE. I just got used to living here. Also, I didn't want to follow up on opportunities to ask about different jobs that could keep me in the UAE. I wasn't ready to leave the summer weather year around. I wasn't ready to leave the cheap flights to other parts of the world I had only imagined. I just wasn't ready, but I had to come to the realization that it was time to go. I asked God many times, "Where are you sending me?" "What do you want me to do?" I was really at a lost for what was going on in my life.

Change is something that can't be avoided. If we live long enough than we will experience change within us and change around us. How we handle the change is what sets us apart from each other. I thought about moving back to Atlanta and just getting a teaching job. However, I just wasn't ready to get back into the game of life. Life is like a game that required endurance, strength, and tenacity. I enjoyed living life on the sideline of the game cheering on my family and friends. I even prayed for my friends while they were running up and down the court. The kickbacks and meetups reminded me of a coach calling a time out and the team huddle together to gain knowledge to play the game. I just wasn't ready to get back in the game starting my day at 6 am and ending a midnight with very few hours of rest. I wasn't ready to give my all to people that didn't consist of my children and get nothing in return. I just didn't understand what was going on.

Could this be my wake-up call to change or a slap in the face. I feel like I had a taste of what was considered the good life that must've been ordained by God himself. Just the thought of going back to my life as I once knew it brought gave me anxiety. While driving, I found it hard to catch my breath. Everything became so heavy. The air became thick, and it was hard for me to swallow. "Slow breaths Theresa," I said to myself. "Take a deep breath, its ok." I thought to myself. I had to talk myself into breathing slowly and steadily. I had a couple moments like that. Was I having an anxiety attack? The last time I experienced those feelings were when my mother was dying from cancer and I was dealing with my divorce. It was my therapist that said I was having an issue with anxiety at that time. However, going abroad helped address my internal issues that brought about anxiety. I was in a space that was able to be still and just listen to my inner being. I learned to take the path of least resistance. I didn't want to row against the current of God's Will.

I had to come to grips that change is inevitable. I believe that people must experience temporary or permanent change in order to be lead to and receive an ultimate victory. Change will lead you to God's calling for your life. If you are not living and working in God's calling for your life, then you're not living. You are just existing in life. When you are living your best life, you will be living an abundant life.

I've noticed a change in Chelsea that I don't think she would have experienced if we had not lived abroad. There is a sense of empowerment and exploration all wrapped up in one that I never had at her age. She is much more willing to explore the world. She is much more aware of the dynamics of law of attraction and prayer than I was at her age. Her brain is constantly thinking of ways to educate and connect people around the world through YouTube, Musically, Instagram, and other technology. She isn't afraid of what people would say or their negative comments. She's definitely a much braver girl.

While things were changing for the expats, things were also changing for the locals. Many of the local administrators were given a severance package without warning that pushed them into early retirement. Their salary was going from 55K AED to 13K AED, and they were not very pleased. This Emiratis spent a lot of money on materialistic items. They didn't have to pay for a home because it was given to them by the government. They spent a lot in the malls on items that were double the price of what I would spend in the U.S. It was like they had nothing better to do with their money other than spend it at the malls. Hence why there were so many massive size malls everywhere. However, some did pay for advanced degrees.

So many people that lived in the UAE for several years said things were changing and that we came in on the tail end of the "good life." I felt like we were getting in on the bottom of a multi-level marketing company. Everything was increasing in pricing. If you wanted to be able to purchase alcohol, you must have a license to purchase and the price of the license was doubling. The speeding tickets had doubled in price. In addition, the municipality fees were increasing. It was like we were paying the government to help take care of their own. This concept was very similar to the United States way of collecting taxes to take care of Americans that were less fortunate. However, there were vast differences.

During preparing to move out of the UAE and looking for a new job, I've become more of aware than ever before when God is sending people and messages into my life. Spending time with the word of God and listening will bring more clarity in your life than ever before. I've posted the sale of many of my furniture items on Facebook. I gave my WhatsApp number for people that were interested. Well one gentleman decides to send me a message asking about the furniture. Then out of nowhere he makes the comment, "You're so beautiful." I then responded back with, "Thank you." I didn't want to seem ungrateful for unappreciative of the comment. So, he asked could he see some of the furniture. I agreed to allow him to come to my villa to look at the furniture. When he arrived, he sent a WhatsApp message that he was outside. Prior to him coming to the house, I sent a message to my two friends that lived in the neighborhood to come over because I didn't trust the guy.

In Arabic countries it is recommended that women should never be alone with men. Chelsea was at my neighbor's house, so I was home alone. In Arabic countries they feel that if a woman is raped because she was alone with a man, then it is her own fault because she should not be alone with a man. Also, some Arabs feel that if a man is alone with a woman she could lie and said he raped her or did something inappropriate. Nonetheless, I didn't want to take the chance. However, by the time he arrived, my neighbors had not responded.

When I opened the door to let him in. He was an attractive man. He was about six feet tall, nice muscular build and had a well-manicured beard. He spoke with an Arabic accent, and his English was understandable. I asked his name and he said Laith. I knew he wasn't an Emirati. He was casually dressed in denim jeans and a striped polo shirt and brown stylish leather loafers. When he entered my villa, he looked at the dining room set, kitchen appliances, and the television. I told him that I didn't have any bedroom furniture to sell. That was not true. I just didn't want him in any of the bedrooms and I was there alone. He asked about the pixels of the television I was selling. I told him that I could check on the box, it was in the back room near the washer and dryer. I was in the middle of washing clothes so when he walked back I saw him looking at panties on the floor. I moved quickly to show him the box that stated the pixels and other features of the television. On the way out, he touched my bra that was hanging on the drying rack in the room which was known as the maid's quarters. He then looked at me and said, "Big." I wasn't shocked because he kept staring at me in a somewhat seductive way. "Ok Laith let's go!" I ushered him back to the living room. He asked about bedroom furniture. I knew my neighbor had a lot of furniture to sell. She had received a termination of contract letter like me. "My friend is around the corner and has furniture to sell would you like to see?" I asked him. He said, "Yes." So, I quickly motioned him out of the door to show him where she lived. "You can ride with me" he insisted. "No, I'm fine. I will show you where she lives." I said. He then walked up to me "You are so beautiful." "Do you not trust me?" He asked. "No, I don't trust you and I don't know you" I said to him as I got in my car. He then got into his white two-door Lexus with dark tinted windows. The tinted windows in this country because of the bright sunlight that drenched the country almost all the time.

When we arrived at my neighbor's house I explained to her what was going on and he allowed her to walk around and look at some of the furniture. I refused to live her by herself. He looked around at the furniture, but he kept looking at me and talking about how beautiful I was. So that only encouraged my girlfriend/neighbor and I to get into his business. He had on a silver ring that resembled a wedding band which prompted me to ask, "Are you married?"

"No."

"So why do you wear a wedding band?"

"I wear it to keep the gay men at my job away."

"What!" "There are gay men at your job"

"Yes, a lot of the Filipino men are gay at my job."

He was quite an attractive man. I could see why the men and women would try to seduce him. Also, there were a lot of gay men living in the UAE. Some of the Filipino men that were gay would be considered to be "flaming" or very feminine.

"So where do you work?" I asked. Even more intrigued.

"I work at the hospital."

"Where are you from?" my friend asked.

"I'm from Jordan" he said.

That explained it all. The men from Jordan were quite flirtations and aggressive as it related to seducing women. During our time in Jordan, the men were quite flirtations and damn near borderline sexual. One of the Jordanian young men asked one of my friends if he could marry her daughter that was on the trip. He was serious. My girlfriend thought it was funny. He offered to pay her in camels, goats, and money.

"So why aren't you married?" I asked.

"I was married for only two months and then she said that she didn't want to be married to me," he said sadly.

It was like she had broken his heart. As my girlfriend and I pried more into his personal business we learned that he was only 30 years old. He married a girl from Oman which was a neighboring country to UAE. He said that he was a virgin up until that point. I felt the conversation moving into a more sexual direction as my friend asked more and more questions about his sexuality. This took a really personal turn. He didn't seem to mind because he wanted sex. He shared that he had only had sex maybe 30 times in his whole life. He shared that he masturbated at least once a day. He said that he had to shower a lot because he could not pray right after sex or masturbation because he would be considered to be unclean in the eyes of Allah. He was a Muslim like most Jordanians.

He shared that one he had been with a Filipino woman and African American woman and he really like the African American woman. We were both shocked. He said that his neighbor a black woman smelled gas at her house, so he went over to check it out. He said she was wearing a really short skirt and she bent over in front of him. After that they had sex. He said she did it all. Oh, did I mention she was a married woman too.

This man said that drinking alcohol and eating pork was "Haram" which means forbidden in Arabic. But, he was willing to fornicate and sleep with a married woman. When I brought it to his attention, he said "I just like sex." When my friend mentioned he could pay for sex he admitted that he had at some of the massage parlors in the UAE. We couldn't believe it! Just like the undercover sex parlors in America, there were some right there in the Holy land of UAE. He further explained that he learned to have sex by looking at pornography. I asked how he looked at pornography when all the sites were blocked in the country. Well he was like most of the people in the country, he had a VPN. Muslims are humans just like Americans. They were dedicated to praying five times a day, but they still committed to sin and did things that were forbidden. I guess they also believed in free will.

He insisted on taking me out on a date, but I declined several times. He openly said that he wanted to have sex with me. Because one African American woman slept with him with no problem he thought we would all sleep with him with no strings attached. I didn't sleep with him and was not interested in sleeping with under no circumstances.

We must live our lives with great expectations and in a way that exhibits what we want. If I want a real relationship then I must live my life in preparation for a relationship, not a one-night stand or a sex partner. Mr. Laith was a horny little Muslim that was seeking many sexual escapes, but he selected the wrong one.

Change is a part of life and if you are not willing to change then be prepared to die. Many people didn't want to accept that the company was going in a different direction and that their jobs with the company were ending. A WhatsApp message was circulating that read,

"This info was sent to me from a friend: Don't ask me any questions because I don't know. I just called and added my name to a list. I spoke with a person form the MOE and "reapplied" or created a case to reapply. What I was told is that the MOE has a window open for anyone who wants to reapply for their jobs. It's a 24-hour period. 8005115. Just call and they'll ask you a few questions about your location, ERP and title. I called at 11:05pm so DO IT NOW!!!"

As I said earlier, I refused to call the number because I knew in my heart and spirt that God's plan was in order and I didn't want to go against them. When God has spoken to you through your heart and spirit and you go against that then you are out of the will of God. Everyone has a different journey in life. Some journeys are long, and some are short.

Living in the UAE and working for Abu Dhabi Education Council was a short journey for me and I could accept that. Unfortunately, other administrators found it very difficult to accept the end of their journey.

When you find it difficult to move forward and accept the end of something, you only make it harder on yourself. As a mother with a daughter watching every move I made I didn't have time to have a pity party. I had to spring into action and remain positive. Ever since Ramadan, I was spending more and more time with the word of God. I felt an increase in my spirituality and the power to really manifest things in my life. I guessed this was the feeling of anointing or having the power to hear from God.

I felt God was communicating with me through the Holy Spirt and through my dreams. I had a dream that I was offered a principalship and before I started the position the school district rescinded the offer. When a person dreams of receiving a job or even losing a job it is a sign of positive changes in finances, responsibility, or warnings that are coming their way. If a person dreams of losing a job, it's an indication of an increase in money or responsibility. I knew that was the spirt of God communicating to me that worrying about a job should be the least of my concerns. He assured me that He was my father and my provider. I needed to relax continue to teach my daughter about the promises and the word of God. The fact that she was learning about the power of God and how He can perform miracles were intriguing to her. After reading about the story of Jesus healing the bleeding woman, she wanted to read and discuss more about Jesus' miracles. I had to remind her that He is still performing miracles today.

CHAPTER 15

CHELSEA RETURNS: UNACCOMPANIED MINOR

Two weeks before the last week of school, I decided to send Chelsea back to America as an unaccompanied minor. This was the end of her time abroad since my contract wasn't terminated. She was one of the few students that was still coming to school and there were only two weeks of school left. I still had another two weeks of school after her and I needed to stay to ensure that the company gave me all the money I was due. The plan was for her to go back with my girlfriend a week earlier, but I waited too late to purchase the ticket and the price had gone up to over fourteen hundred USD. Then, I told her that we would go to Egypt before we left after I got out of school. But, that meant that she wouldn't have a summer break. She'd much rather go home early and have a summer vacation than to go to Egypt. At 11 years old, I would've done the same thing.

Before her flight left we met friends for dinner and dessert at the mall. These were friends Chelsea and I considered newest family members. It was like everybody loved Chelsea. Most of the people knew Chelsea before they met me from her bubbly personality at the hotel when we first moved to UAE. It didn't take long before the tears started to flow as we realized that it would be the last time Chelsea would be visiting Al Ain Mall. The kids and the adults all hugged Chelsea and said they would miss her. My friend Tasha even gave her 50 Dirhams to buy something on her way home.

I couldn't hold back the tears as I drove my baby girl to the airport to take an international flight home by herself. I was so proud of her. She wasn't the least bit afraid. She sat in the sit with such confidence and talked about how she wouldn't hear the only pop radio station anymore. We both reminisced about how brave she had become over the past year. She said, "Mommy, I've rode a donkey, a horse, and an elephant." She was right too! All the adventures and travel and matured my little girl and gave her a brave heart.

After checking in we were introduced to a Filipino lady that would accompany Chelsea through immigration and on to her flight. I had to say my last good bye at the walkway about 10 yards from the immigration counters. We hugged, and the tears began to fall from our eyes. "I'm so very proud of you Chelsea and thank you for going on this journey with me," I said through my tears. "I love you so much and remember to message me" I added. Earlier that week we downloaded Facebook on her tablet, so she could send me messages. We even practiced the process around the house. I gave her my credit card information to buy Wi-Fi on the plane.

I cried all the way on home from the airport. I looked over at the empty seat where my baby girl was just sitting. "God it hurts so bad" I said as the tears ran down my fat cheeks. "Please protect my baby girl" I said. I didn't understand this transition period in my life. On the way, I felt the urge to listen to Fred Hammonds song, "Trust in the Lord." I knew that was God reminding me to trust him and not try to understand what was happening. I learned to listen to the desires of my heart and soul because those were messages from God.

Chelsea finally sent me a message that read, "I'm on the plane" "Hi" "I'm in Paris right now." All the messages came through at one time. "Hi baby girl!" "How was your flight?" I responded. She quickly responded back, "Good. I met new friends in the kids' solo club." Before I could ask where the children were from, she texted again, "They're French." I had to chuckle a little because it was like she knew me so well. She then video called me on messenger. She wanted to talk to me and show me the kids solo club. She panned the camera as she pointed out the kids play area, a television, the sitting area, and the breakfast area where there were drinks and croissants. She was not afraid at all and her face was void of tears unlike mine. I told her to ask the flight attendant to help her connect to the Wi-Fi and use my credit card number I had written down.

I couldn't stop crying at work all day. It was like I was an emotional mess. Several of the teachers asked about Chelsea. "I prayed for your daughter" "She will be fine, Inshallah." Her layover in Paris was only 3 hours.

As I was attending a wedding my U.S. phone rang showing a Colombia, South Carolina number. \

"Hello, may I speak with Ms. Theresa Brown."

"Yes."

"This is …from Delta Airlines."

My heart immediately stopped and then started pumping extremely fast. I immediately thought to myself, could something have happened to my little girl?

"I'm calling because I wanted to inform you that Chelsea's flight had to be diverted to South Carolina because of the weather in Atlanta." "I wanted to be the first to let you know." I immediately became sick to my stomach. I was so mad that I didn't get her a little cheap phone to call me in case of emergency. We were relying on internet and Facebook messenger. I gave her my credit card information and told her to ask the flight attendant to help her, so she could purchase Wi-Fi. I could kick myself for that mistake. I told the representative to contact her father because he was at the airport expecting her.

I texted her dad to follow up. Chelsea arrived in Atlanta a few hours later than what was expected due to the weather. When I finally talked to her she was so excited to be home. She said the number didn't work for her to purchase Wi-Fi. She said that she tore up the paper with my credit card information and put it in the trash.

After hanging up with her, I couldn't help but think about how mature she sounded. My little girl was really changing physically and maturing mentally. She hadn't started her menstruation, but she her body was showing signs of puberty being introduce to her. She was no longer the little girl I brought to the United Arab Emirates eleven months ago.

Our experiences had changed us into the young lady she was becoming and woman I was today. I understood more now than ever before that I had to power and ability to create a life that I wanted for me. I no longer had to accept lies from a man just to say that I had a boyfriend, knowing that he was a liar and a cheat. I no longer had to beg a company for a job because I understood where my help came from. I no longer had to stay in a place that I wasn't wanted because I knew where I was welcomed. I understood that life's journey isn't a destination, but a process and personal path that can be created.

CHAPTER 16

EXIT PROCESS

The exit process is about as tedious as the entrance process. The Ministry of Education has a process for exiting the company that is simple, but tedious. The company holds your last two paychecks until you have checked out completely. Yes, they hold your last two paychecks until you have completely checked out. The first step to checking out is to complete all the housing requirements. The housing requirements includes moving completely out of your apartment, flat, or villa.

I sold most of my furniture. I hired a shipping company to ship my bedroom set, dining room set and a few odds and ends. The cost of shipping my items to the United States costs me thirteen thousand dirhams, which is about three thousand five hundred USD. I should've had them ship all my dishes too. But, I didn't. I had to go through the hassle of selling them and getting rid of them. I paid six hundred dirhams which was $163 USD to two maintenance guys to paint my villa back to the original color. I just painted my villa two months prior to getting the termination letter. However, I wanted to get my deposit back from the management company. My deposit was 6200 dirhams, which was about $1600 USD. I needed all my money back. So, it took a good month to sell and move my things out of my villa.

After everything was out and cleaned up, I requested the power to be turned off. I made a mistake and requested that the power be turned off too soon. When I came home from work one afternoon, there was no power. It was 110 degrees outside. I couldn't believe they turned the power off so soon. When I called the representative said it would be several days before they turned it off. I thought perfect I would be out by then. So, when I got home to no power days before the expected shut off date, I broke down. I cried in my car with the air on in the drive way. I had no job leads in the U.S., Chelsea was gone home, and I thought about how Jesus must've felt on the cross when he said, "My God, my God, why have you forsaken me?" I had to remember that God would not put more on me than I could bear.

I called the power company in tears and sweat pouring down my face. I asked if they could turn the power back on because it was shut off too soon. The man on the phone in his Arabic voice said it would take days. "I would be dead from the heat by then," I cried out. I then requested to speak with a supervisor. He put me on hold for two minutes which seemed like twenty minutes and said, "A supervisor will call you back." I went to my friend's house that lived a few doors down. The supervisor called me back within 30 minutes and said that a technician would be out within three hours to turn the power back on. The power was back on within two hours.

The process of selling my furniture was a tremendous hurdle. My furniture and appliances were less than a year old and still under warranty. Most of the people that came to look at the kitchen appliances were from Egypt and Jordan. They wanted to ship the appliance to their home country. Therefore, they didn't care if the appliances were under warranty or how old they were. They wanted to buy them for pennies. However, the items that were sold went to people that were still living in UAE and had not planned to ship them anywhere. One lady even bought some of my groceries that you could only find in America. She was from America and wasn't planning to go home for a while.

The next step after moving everything out was getting a clearance letter from the housing management company to say that I didn't owe them any money or have any damages. Then I could get the power, water, and cable turned off. Because I was only in the country for one year, the cable company charged me 3153 AED ($858 USD) for early termination of the contract and one month of service even though I only used 2 days. I then had to wait one week before I could receive a clearance letter from the cable company. When I asked why it took so long, the gentleman stated that they had to process hundreds of clearance letters and it would take time. He stated that this happens every year around the same time. I couldn't help but think why the company wouldn't come up with a more efficient way to process the letters. Then I realized, they didn't have to because people didn't complain, and they were owned by the government. I had to have a clearance letter from the power company, cable company, and housing management company to give to my employer to get my last two pay checks and flight allowance for Chelsea and me. My bonus for one year of service would not be received because I had to pay back a portion of the furniture allowance since I didn't stay pass the one year.

Moving out of my villa was not as hard as it was when I moved out of my apartment in Atlanta. I still had a lot of clothes because I brought back three large suitcases full of clothes when I went home in December. I managed to get all my things to take home in six large suitcases. Once I moved out of my villa, I moved in with my linesister to wait for the company to process everything. I was lucky to have friends that would allow me to stay with them. Many people had to pay for a hotel and wait to be processed. In the past, the company would put people in a hotel for one to two weeks while they were processed out. This year the company was not paying for people to stay in a hotel.

Chelsea would call and check up on me every day. She would leave me voice messages on Facebook messenger. I was so touched by her messages and was so thankful. One of her messages said, "Are you ok? Are you praying? Are you motivating yourself? Just stay positive, stay positive mom!" To hear her say that was like God was sending me a message to stay motivated and stay positive. In addition, to the housing tasks, I had to cancel Chelsea's visa that costs 102 AED ($30 USD). That was the easiest process of them all.

The biggest hurdle of exiting was getting the housing complex to sign the housing clearance form. I paid a shipping a little over 13000 AED ($3000 USD) company to pack most of my things to ship back to America. I couldn't give them an address for shipping because I didn't have a home. Technically, I was homeless in UAE and USA. It seemed like I was in bad shape, but I had faith that things would work out for my good and my benefit.

The housing manager was on vacation so the person that was filling in for her wasn't available for the second day in a row. I was getting more and more frustrated in the 110-degree heat. When I contacted the substitute manager by phone he said, "Today is ladies day at the clubhouse and I couldn't enter the premises." "Well I need this form signed and stamped. I'm leaving the country tomorrow morning" I yelled. I wasn't leaving the next day, but I needed him to move with a sense of urgency. No one in the country especially in Sleepy Town Al Ain moved with any urgency. I had to wait until 10:30 that morning until "Ladies Time" was up. I finally was able to make my way to turn all the paperwork in to the Al Ain office of Abu Dhabi Education Council. It took me an entire day to finally gather the necessary paperwork to close out everything and ensure my compensation.

After turning in the paperwork, I felt a sense of relief and a slight attitude at the same time. All the necessary paperwork including the cancellation of my visa was complete. I now had 30 days to exit the country without any penalties or fines from the government and I had four school days left. Here I was a 43-year-old woman with four college degrees and 20 years of successful educational experience terminated for the first time in my life. I thought, "Who the hell did they think they were?" "Did they not know the prize possession they hired and let go in one year?" T.D. Jakes had to remind me that sometimes God will stir up things in your life to move you to something better. That same night I received an Instagram message that read:

Dr. Brown, you don't know me and probably don't remember. My name is -----. I wished you well on your endeavors before leaving Perkerson. I was there as a parent then, I'm there as a Para now. I just wanted to reach out to you first and foremost to say as a black woman, I'm proud of you. They were like Dr. Brown is living her best life, and I'm like DR. BROWN IS THE SHIT!!! I just admire you and I look from far. I have a long road ahead and so many of us don't like to help each other or share "the plug," and I just get so discouraged sometimes. Seeing your posts have kept me motivated and I'm just trying to be a bigger and better version of me. I just wanted to say Hi. Keep living your best life!

Receiving that message let me know that someone is always watching, and I could inspire someone other than my children to be great and live their best life. I realized that I was exiting one journey and entering another journey of the unknown. However, my next journey didn't have the same me. I was a new me with a new mindset. I learned to trust God and my inner self. I knew that my next journey was bigger than me. It was about overcoming fear, self-love, inspiration, and more importantly faith. Faith and fear can't dominate the mind at the same time. I had to allow faith to occupy my total being and listen to myself.

When things got tough and I didn't know what was going on in a meeting and I felt isolated, I learned that it was God's way of getting me to turn to him. When I broke down because I missed my son and questioned my motherhood, it was God's way of getting me to turn to him. When things were bleak because I didn't know where I would be employed the next school year, it was God's way of getting me to turn to him. I even asked God, "Show me a sign that you haven't forgotten about me. I still need a job." Within a couple hours later, I received an email about a job interview. It was God's way of letting me know that he was still on the throne and that he had a plan for my life.

My mother would always say, "Everybody is not your friend." I realized that I must surround myself around positive motivating sources. It is scientifically proven, a person that is in your presence that is negative and miserable can affect your mood and energy and not have to say a word to you. Personal and professional association is key. The best grade level teams were the ones in which the teachers worked collectively in a harmonious environment. Napoleon Hill said it best, "The wise man never wastes his time with anyone form whom he can not acquire benefits or to whom he cannot contribute something worthwhile in one form or another. I learned to stop wasting energy with people that didn't align to God's purpose and plan for my life.

The last day of school was bittersweet. I was so ready to go home to see my children and get out of the hot temperatures. The temperature rose to 120 degrees. The staff went around hugging one another. I became filled with emotion as I hugged the Tea Girl, Jenny. She was one of the hardest working people at the school. Daily she served me coffee, tea, sandwiches, and a warm smile. When I saw the finance manager, Meena come into Queen's office as we finished taking pictures I hugged her so tight and begin to cry again. I thought about how she helped me navigate the school's bookkeeping side of things. She was so open with me and translated everything for me.

I promised to stop by the salon to say good bye to my Nigerian hair stylist, Cynthia. She was so happy to see me she immediately hugged me and began to cry. She hugged me like I was family. In some kind of way, we were all family. We were all women from different backgrounds and different countries that became like family. I gave items to Cynthia without her asking because I knew she needed them. She walked me to the car and got into the car and to my hands and begin to pray for me. She prayed over me like never before. She asked God to increase me and strengthen me. The tears rolled down my cheeks as I heard the words flow naturally from her mouth. I knew God heard her prayers as we held hands and humbly said, "Amen" at the same time.

The entire day was so emotional. I was hurting because I knew that would be the last time, I would see my coworkers and stylist ever again. We all knew that God had spoken and that it was time for me to move into my next assignment. It didn't feel good. It reminded me of the time that I transferred Chelsea from Parkside Elementary to our neighborhood school in Rockdale County. At the time, she was in first grade and there were just too many incidents that were occurring, and it was weighing heavy on Chelsea. She was not acting like herself or the child that I was raising.

I cried the entire weekend because I knew Parkside was a good school, but it wasn't a fit for Chelsea. I had handpicked all her teachers, so I knew she would get the academics she needed. However, the dynamics of the school were changing, and Chelsea was becoming something that I didn't like. Once I transferred her to the neighborhood school, it was like a burden had been lifted off her. She felt more like a first grader instead of constantly trying to compete with the gifted students or fit in with kids that had different experiences and backgrounds.

I had that same feeling in the pit of my soul. It was like God knew that this assignment did what it was supposed to do and now it was time to move on to my purpose. I could see more clearly that some people assignment required people to be removed from their lives so that God could work on them. Deirdre and my neighbor Meron hated that Chelsea and I would no longer be around, but their assignment and purpose called for our absence. God has a special way of moving things around and people around to help us get into His will and obtain perfect peace.

So many times, we are trained to listen to others and not trained to listen to ourselves. I had spent a year living abroad and traveling to learn how to appreciate life and acceptance.

I learned how to accept my daughter for whom God was transforming. I learned to live without a man in my life. I learned how to live without having sexual intercourse on a regular basis. I learned to accept and live with other cultures and races. More importantly, I learned to love me.

Loving me involved accepting who I was and allowing myself time to be with just me. I had time to think about my life and the things that I perceived to me mistakes that weren't mistakes at all. It was God's way of preparing me to live out his plan and accepting his creation of me. I didn't have to take time; it was like time was there waiting for me to use it to discover me.

This specific journey may have come to an end, but there is still more to come in my journey of life. I realize that things will happen in life that will push you to uncomfortable places and situations. However, extraordinary things can't happen when you live an ordinary life. I didn't allow fear to stop me from moving to the United Arab Emirates and traveling to other countries with my 11-year-old daughter. So, I end this journey as a more confident woman that is spiritually satisfied, and more fulfilled by His grace.

ABOUT THE AUTHOR

Dr. Theresa Brown is an author, trainer, speaker, coach, and the mother of two children Chelsea (12) and Rylan (7). She is the Chief Executive Officer of High Performance Consultants LLC where she enjoys providing leadership training and coaching to individuals, groups, and organizations. She has over 20 years of experience in education in which the last decade has been in school administration. Her work includes national presentations at the New Teacher Center Symposium, Atlanta Public Schools: New Teacher Seminar: Assessing All Learners and Effective Classroom Environment, National Council of English Teachers Conference, and College Board Conference: A Dream Deferred: The Future of African Americans. The Detroit native believes focusing on professional and personal growth and development is the key to living intentionally. Dr. Brown thoroughly believes that adding value to people and providing professional and personal development is the key to creating a leadership culture that values people.

She has a Doctorate degree in Instructional Leadership, a master's degree in Curriculum and Instruction, and a Bachelor's degree in Elementary Education. She's taught elementary and middle school and served as an Instructional Mentor to novice teachers, and an Instructional coach for Atlanta Public Schools. In addition, she served as an Evaluator for Western Governors University.